The Prophecy of Saint Malachy
The Soon Coming End of Days

by Joseph Lumpkin

Joseph Lumpkin

The Prophecy of Malachy:
The Soon Coming End of Days
by Joseph Lumpkin

Copyright © 2012

All rights reserved.

Fifth Estate Publishers

2795 County Hwy 57

Blountsville, AL 35031.

First Printing 2012

Cover art by An Quigley

Printed on acid-free paper

Library of Congress Control No: 2012935973
ISBN: 9781936533244

Fifth Estate

The Prophecy Of Saint Malachy
The Soon Coming End of Days

The events of 1978 saw the death of Pope Paul VI, the election and unexpected death of John Paul I, and finally the election of John Paul II. Three Popes in one year propelled the world like a runaway train toward the conclusion of a prophecy given by St. Malachy in 1139. The prophecy lists 112 Popes. The last Pope would take the seat of Saint Peter and the world would fall into anarchy. John Paul II was the 110th Pope. The Pope ruling the Holy See today is Benedict XVI, the 111th Pope, and according to the prophecy, the last Pope to rule an intact church and functioning world. The next Pope will not be the Vicar of Christ. He will be the enemy of the church, usurper of the throne and he will be called "Peter of Rome."

The ominous prophecy has echoed through the centuries for over 870 years:

In persecutione extrema S.R.E. sedebit Petrus Romanus, qui pascet oves in multis tribulationibus: quibus transactis civitas septicollis

3

diruetur,
& Judex tremêdus judicabit populum suum. Finis.

(In extreme persecution, the seat of the Holy Roman Church will be occupied by Peter the Roman, who will feed the sheep through many tribulations, at the term (end) of which the city of seven hills (Rome) will be destroyed, and the formidable Judge will judge his people.)

Saint Malachy's prophecy foretells the succession of Roman Catholic Popes from Celestine II [1143 AD] to John Paul II's successor, Saint Benedict XVI, who sits in the Chair of Saint Peter today. Malachy wrote that he was describing the pontiffs from Celestine II "...to the end of the world." At the end of the world, Malachy declared that Rome will be destroyed and God will judge his people. Was Malachy a prophet or madman?

Who Was Saint Malachy?

In 1094 A.D. the noble family of O'Morgair in Armagh, in what is now Northern Ireland, was blessed with an heir. A son was born into this family of noble, wealthy, landowners. The child was baptized with the name "Maelmhaedhoc."

When the child was old enough to leave the family and start his education he was placed under the tutorship of Imbar O'Hagan in the Abby at Armagh. It was at this time his name was changed. Latin was the language of the church and so Maelmhaedhoc's name would be Latinized. His name would now be Malachy. Later, after he became well known, his Irish descendants would adopt that same baptismal name of Malachy as the family's surname.

It was customary at the time for many wealthy families to have a son in the clergy, thus, after Malachy's education his father decided he should become a Roman Catholic priest. He was ordained in 1119 AD at the age of 25. His "secular" education would not be enough for the role he would play and so his theological education would commence in Lismore.

Malachy, was appointed as Abbot of Bangor in 1123. A year later he was consecrated as the Archbishop of Connor. In 1127 he became "father confessor" to Cormac MacCarthy, Prince of Desmond, who would later become the King of Ireland.
In 1132 he was promoted to the primacy of Armagh. Armagh is a county with a city by the same name, which at one time was a hot bed of Pagan practice. Its Archdiocese was founded by St. Patrick in 445 as the primatial See of Ireland.. It is now divided into 55 parishes.

After taking his place in Armagh, Malachy suffered many tribulations as he tried to effect a reformation in the diocese. He resigned the See after three years and retired to the Bishopric of

Down. In 1139 he went to Rome and solicited the Pope for two palliums, one for the See of Armagh and the other probably for the new Metropolitan See of Cashel.

The pallium, derived from the Roman pallium or palla. It is a woolen cloak, which is an ecclesiastical vestment originally peculiar to the Pope. There was a time lasting several centuries in which it was bestowed by the Pope on metropolitans and primates as a symbol of their authority and jurisdiction delegated to them by the Holy See.

A metropolitan is a bishop who has authority over bishops in a province. Likewise, a primate is a chief bishop or archbishop of an area.
In the years that followed, Malachy introduced the Cistercian Order into Ireland by the advice of St. Bernard.

It was during a visit to the Pope that Malachy would receive a vision, which would span centuries. The vision and prophecy was of a line of men that would occupy the Seat of Saint Peter, ruling and residing over the Roman Catholic Church. Historians believe that Malachy received his papal succession vision during his visit to Rome in 1140 for the coronation of Innocent II. Malachy gave the recorded vision to the new pontiff to "comfort him in his afflictions." Innocent II placed the document in the papal archive where it remained for four centuries, read only by the curator of the library and other high-ranking church officials.

Later, as his legend grew it would be reported that in addition to the gift of prophecy Malachy had the gift of healing the sick. Some said he possessed the powers of levitation and clairvoyance. Numerous miracles are attributed to his ministry.

His prophesies concerned the succession of the Popes from Pope Innocent II to the Pope who will follow John Paul II, which will be the Pope who either precedes the end or reigns at the end. According to his prophecy, the line of Popes will end abruptly with the next Pope either after the pontiff whose motto is "The Glory of the Olive," which many think is the symbol of peace. Thus, the Pope who becomes the one to reconcile the church to its enemies will be the herald of the end. It is said that during his reign, peace will descend over the Mideast.

Here the prophecy becomes slightly confusing. Later versions of Malachy's prophecy lists 112 Popes while earlier versions have 111 Popes. There is also some confusion as to if the Pope following John Paul II is the terminus or if he is the penultimate. Either way, it cannot be stressed enough that we are now at the end of this prophecy and we are witnessing either the reign of the last Pope or the reign of the one who will prepare the way for him.

Malachy wrote that he was describing the pontiffs from Celestine II "...to the end of the world." In a vision the Holy Spirit revealed each future pontiff by his character, geographic or physiological attributes, or his coat of arms.

Malachy died on his second pilgrimage to Rome in 1148. He was canonized by Pope Clemente III on July 6, 1199. Among Malachy's prophesies was his prediction of the day and hour of his own death, which proved accurate.

Although it appears that Malachy's original prophecy contained 111 Popes, in the 1820 printed version of Malachy's prophesies, Lignum Vitre (written in 1559 by a Benedictine historian, Arnold Wyon), a 112th Pope appears that was not in Malachy's original manuscript. The 112th Pope was likely added by the Olivetan monks. The Order of St. Benedict claims this final Pope will come within the Benedictine Order, and that he was placed in the succession line because St. Benedict himself prophesied that before the end of the world, his Order will triumphantly lead the Catholic Church in its battle against evil (the Battle of Armageddon). Was St. Benedict's "prophecy" from a heavenly revelation or was it more ego and wishful thinking than spiritual insight? One never knows about such things until hindsight overtakes us.

Malachy does not list Popes from the beginning of the church, only those from Celestine II, who was the Pope coming after the one in office when Malachy died. This means his first prophecy begins with the 167th Pope of the church and ends with Pope number 267. "Anti-Popes" are also listed, making up the full list from Celestine II to the end of days. The last prophecy was added after Malachy completed his prophetic writing.

An anti-Pope is one who falsely claims the title and authority of the Holy Father while a duly elected Pope is in office. I have included in this list only anti-Popes who have had at least some pretence of being canonically elected. Impostors whose only claim to the Papal office was having received an alleged divine revelation appointing them Pope are not considered "genuine" anti-Popes and are thus omitted from numbering, although they are listed.

The List of Anti-Popes was taken from JND Kelly's THE OXFORD DICTIONARY OF POPES (Oxford University Press: 1986, 1988). This book was chosen as an unbiased and neutral source.

List of Anti-Popes
217-235 St. Hippolytus. One of the Fathers of the Church and the only anti-Pope to be venerated as a saint. Elected "Pope" in opposition to St. Callistus I (r. 217-222) whom he accused of being a Monarchian heretic. The schism continued in opposition to Urban I (r. 222-230) and St. Pontian (r. 230-235). The Imperial gov't, during the persecution of Emp. Maximin Thrax, exiled both

Hippolytus and Pontian to Sardinia, where they were reconciled. Apparently, to end the schism they both abdicated.

251-258 Novatian. Consecrated bishop in opposition to St. Cornelius (r. 251-253). The major point in dispute (besides disappointed ambition on Novatian's part) was his opposition to the policy St. Cornelius pursued as regarded those Christians who lapsed during the persecution of Emperor Decius. The Pope insisted on restoring the "lapsi" to communion after doing suitable penance. Novatian demanded permanent excommunication from the Church.

309 Heraclius

355-365 Felix II

366-367 Ursinus

418-419 Eulalius

498-505 Laurentius

687 Theodore

687 Paschal

767-769 Constantine

768 Philip

844 John

855 Anastasius the Librarian. One of the more interesting anti-Popes. A scholar learned in both Greek and Latin. After the death of St. Leo IV in 855, Anastasius, with Frankish support, tried to make himself Pope in rivalry to the lawful Pope Benedict III (r. 855-858). The violent hostility of the Romans thwarted him. Anastasius was treated leniently by Benedict and rehabilitated by Nicholas I (r. 858-867), whom he served faithfully.

903-904 Christopher

984-985 Boniface VII. One of the more disgusting anti-Popes. Actually, twice anti-Pope. In 974, supported by the Roman clan of the Crescentii, Boniface was "elected" Pope. He soon had the lawful Pope Benedict VI (r. 973-974) murdered. The outraged Romans expelled Boniface, who fled to the Eastern Roman Empire. In 980, while Benedict VII (r. 974-983) was absent, the usurper briefly seized Rome. Again expelled. In 984, with Byzantine support, Boniface again seized Rome, had John XIV (r. 983-984) murdered, and installed himself as "Pope" until he died in 985.
997-998 John XVI
1012 Gregory
1045 Sylvester III. Scholars debate over whether or not he was truly an anti-Pope.
1058-1059 Benedict X
1061-1072 Honorius II
1084-1100 Clement III
1100 Theodoric
1102 Albert
1105-1111 Sylvester IV
1118-1121 Gregory VIII
1124 Celestine II
1130-1138 Anacletus II
1138 Victor IV
1159-1164 Victor IV. The anti-Popes of the years 1159-1180 were the creations of the Holy Roman Emperor Frederick I during his long quarrel with Pope Alexander III (r. 1159-1181).
1164-1168 Paschal III
1168-1178 Callistus III
1179-1180 Innocent III

1328-1330 Nicholas V. Set up as anti-Pope by the Holy Roman Emperor Louis IV during the latter's quarrel with Pope John XXII (r. 1316-1334).
1378-1394 Clement VII. The "election" of this anti-Pope in opposition to the lawful Pope Urban VI (r. 1378-1389) precipitated the Western Schism of 1378-1415.
1394-1423 Benedict XIII
1049-1410 Alexander V
1410-1415 John XXIII
1423-1429 Clement VIII
1425-1430 Benedict XIV
1439-1449 Felix V. After "deposing" Eugene IV (r. 1431-1447) in 1439, the schismatic Council of Basle "elected" as "Pope" Amadeus VIII, Duke of Savoy (r. 1391-1440. Largely because the "council" desired as Pope a man of piety, wealth, and international standing. Amadeus accepted "election" only with hesitation and was soon disillusioned. In 1449, with Charles VII of France acting as mediator, Felix V submitted to the lawful Pope Nicholas V. Appointed cardinal bishop of St. Sabina, he died in 1451.

Out of the above list, Malachy lists those who disrupted the papacy within the years he lists in the chronology between Celestine II (1143-1144) and the end of days. All Anti-Popes occur between 1159 and 1449. After the Protestant Reformation was underway the Catholic Church and its political processes became more consolidated. World political structures no longer set Emperors and Popes at odds enough to split kingdoms or churches. Divisions at the higher levels within the church never gave way to another Anti-Pope.

There has been some conjecture that the prophecies were not written by Malachy, but were written instead by a Cardinal named Simoncelli. However, Vatican records show that the document was entrusted to Innocent II in 1140. Like many other important Vatican documents, the Malachy Prophecy was later printed on the Gutenberg Press in 1455, which was 135 years before Cardinal Simoncelli supposedly wrote them. Malachy's Prophecy was unknown outside the church hierarchy but printed copies of the prophecy were in circulation before 1590.

In Malachy's prophecy the future pontiffs were identified by their origins, their family crest or coat of arms, a key event in their personal history, or sweeping religious or political changes which occurred while the Pope was in office. The description or attributes of the man or his time in office became known as his Motto.

Here are some examples:

Clement XIII (1758 and 1769), had close ties with the Italian state of Umbria, whose State emblem was the rose. Malachy referred to him as the "Rosa Umbriae," or the "Rose of Umbria."

Pius II had the second shortest reign and was Pope for only 26 days in 1503. His family name was Piccolomini, which is Italian for "little man." He was described in Malachy's prophecy as "De Parvo Homine" (From a little man). Cardinal Giovanni Anngelico Braschi, had the longest period as Pope. He lived 82 years and served as pontiff for over half his life. He was installed in 1755 and served until his death in 1799, which was period of 44 years. Contemporary Christian writers refer to Pius VI as the Apostolic Pilgrim on Earth. Malachy described him as the pilgrim Pope.

There are instances where political intrigue or upheaval overshadowed or influenced the day. Pius VII, whose name was Barnaba Chiaramonte, was named Pope Pius VI in 1786 in the shadow of the rise in power of Napoleon Bonaparte. His pontificate was symbolized by the eagle, which was the symbol of Napoleon and his empire.

Pope Leo XIII [1878-1903] was given the motto in the papal prophecy of "Lumen in Caelo" (Light in the Heavens). Real name: Gioacchio Vincenzo Raffaele. His coat of arms depicted a shooting star.

Pope Pius X [1903-1914] was entitled "Ignis Ardens" (Burning Fire). Real name: Giuseppe Melchiarre Sarto. It was during Sarto's reign that Europe burst in war, which spread from one nation to another until 1914, when war devoured the entire continent.

Benedict XV [1914-1922] "Religio Depopulata" (Religion Devastated) Real name: Giacomo Della Chiesa. Benedict XV was witness to the rise of secular and non-religious viewpoint, giving way to the concept of the New World Order. Talk of the New order included a single, united government, people, and economy. Some feared this was the tide and course mentioned in Revelation 13 (one world government), Revelation 17 (the one world church) and Revelation 18 (the one world economy).

Pope Pius XI [1922-1939] Real name: Achilee Ratti. His motto was "Fides Intrepida" (Unshaken Faith). Ratti witnessed the preparation for another world war and the discarding of religion by some. Europe saw an abortion movement and the rise of secularism, which was a world view dismissing religion. The philosophical view was taught in the major colleges and universities with an eye toward the emerging New World Order.

Pope Pius XII [1939-1958]— Born Eugento Pacelli "Pastor Angelicus" (Angelic Shepherd). He was a diplomat for the Vatican. 1917 - 1929, he served in Nuncio, Germany. In 1930 he became Vatican Secretary of State. He was an experienced leader, wise enough to deal with Kings, Presidents, and the Church, even during a global conflict.

15

Knowing the prophecies, some men have attempted to artificially conform to the mottos of Malachy. In an unabashedly arrogant attempt to use the prophecy to his own ends, Cardinal Spellman did the ridiculous. In 1958, before the Conclave that would elect Pope John XXIII, Cardinal Spellman of New York hired a boat, filled it with sheep and sailed up and down the Tiber River in a show of symbolism aimed at Malachy's prophecies. He wished to show that he was "pastor et nautor" (pastor and sailor), the motto attributed to the next Pope in the prophecies. Obviously, Spellman was passed over.

Pope John XXIII [1958-1963] Born as Angelo Giuseppe Roncalli Motto: "Pastor et nauta" (Pastor and mariner) Roncalli spent several years as the apostolic delegate and Nuncio in Turkey, Greece, Bulgaria and France. Roncalli was named Archbishop of Areoplis (Rabbath and Moah) in Palestine around the birth of Israel in 1948.

In 1953 Pope Pius XII named him as the Cardinal of Venice. He was viewed, at the time, as the most beloved of all modern Popes. That was, of course, until the pontificating of Karol Wojtyla, the Polish prince of the church, John Paul II. Roncalli fulfilled the Malachy Prophecy as the "mariner" through his tenure in Venice. Venice uses canals for transportation. It is the water city filled with boats called Gondolas.

Pope Paul VI [1953-1968] Born as Giovanni Battista Montini. Motto: Flos Florum" (Flower of flowers). His reign as pontiff was only five years. His power came in the Catholic Church through the office of the Vatican Secretary of State. Cardinals elected him Pope in 1953. The coat of arms of the Montini family depicts three fleurs-de-lis.

Pope John Paul I [1978-1978 (34 days)]— "DeMedietate lunae" (of the half moon). Real name: Albino Buciani. His reign was the second shortest in papal history. It was because of the briefness of his tenure that Wojtyla took the papal name, John Paul II. During the brief reign of John Paul I, the rise of Muslim extremism against the Gentile world exploded and OPEC (Oil Producing Exporting Countries) was born. The symbol of the Muslim world is the crescent—the half moon.

Pope John Paul II [1978-2005]—"De Lobaore solis" (Of the eclipse of the sun) or (from the toil of the sun.) was beloved by all. Over 3 million people have traveled to Rome to pay their last respects to the fallen pontiff who mastered 8 languages but spoke 20 as he evangelized the world for Christ. Karol Wojtyla came from the working class in Poland. There were 16 solar eclipses that were visible from southern Europe during his time. This is not so unusual. If one

17

artisans from Rimsting on the shore of Lake Chiem, and before marrying she worked as a cook in a number of hotels.

He spent his childhood and adolescence in Traunstein, a small village near the Austrian border, thirty kilometres from Salzburg. In this environment, which he himself has defined as "Mozartian", he received his Christian, cultural and human formation.

His youthful years were not easy. His faith and the education received at home prepared him for the harsh experience of those years during which the Nazi regime pursued a hostile attitude toward the Catholic Church. The young Joseph saw how some Nazis beat the Parish Priest before the celebration of Mass.

It was precisely during that complex situation that he discovered the beauty and truth of faith in Christ; fundamental for this was his family's attitude, who always gave a clear witness of goodness and hope, rooted in a convinced attachment to the Church.

During the last months of the war he was enrolled in an auxiliary anti-aircraft corps. From 1946 to 1951 he studied philosophy and theology in the Higher School of Philosophy and Theology of Freising and at the University of Munich.

He received his priestly ordination on 29 June

1951. A year later he began teaching at the Higher School of Freising. In 1953 he obtained his doctorate in theology with a thesis entitled "People and House of God in St Augustine's Doctrine of the Church".

Four years later, under the direction of the renowned professor of fundamental theology Gottlieb Söhngen, he qualified for University teaching with a dissertation on: "The Theology of History in St Bonaventure".

After lecturing on dogmatic and fundamental theology at the Higher School of Philosophy and Theology in Freising, he went on to teach at Bonn, from 1959 to1963; at Münster from 1963 to 1966 and at Tübingen from 1966 to 1969. During this last year he held the Chair of dogmatics and history of dogma at the University of Regensburg, where he was also Vice-President of the University.

From 1962 to 1965 he made a notable contribution to Vatican II as an "expert"; being present at the Council as theological advisor of Cardinal Joseph Frings, Archbishop of Cologne.

His intense scientific activity led him to important positions at the service of the German Bishops' Conference and the International Theological Commission.

In 1972 together with Hans Urs von Balthasar, Henri de Lubac and other important theologians, he initiated the theological journal "Communio".

On 25 March 1977 Pope Paul VI named him Archbishop of Munich and Freising. On 28 May of the same year he received episcopal ordination. He was the first Diocesan priest for 80 years to take on the pastoral governance of the great Bavarian Archdiocese. He chose as his episcopal motto: "Cooperators of the truth". He himself explained why: "On the one hand I saw it as the relation between my previous task as professor and my new mission. In spite of different approaches, what was involved, and continued to be so, was following the truth and being at its service. On the other hand I chose that motto because in today's world the theme of truth is omitted almost entirely, as something too great for man, and yet everything collapses if truth is missing".

Paul VI made him a Cardinal with the priestly title of "Santa Maria Consolatrice al Tiburtino", during the Consistory of 27 June of the same year.

In 1978 he took part in the Conclave of 25 and 26 August which elected John Paul I, who named him his Special Envoy to the III International Mariological Congress, celebrated in Guayaquil (Ecuador) from 16 to 24 September. In the month of October of the same year he took part in the Conclave that elected Pope John Paul II.

He was Relator of the V Ordinary General Assembly of the Synod of Bishops which took place in 1980 on the theme: "Mission of the

Christian Family in the world of today", and was Delegate President of the VI Ordinary General Assembly of 1983 on "Reconciliation and Penance in the mission of the Church".

John Paul II named him Prefect of the Congregation for the Doctrine of the Faith and President of the Pontifical Biblical Commission and of the International Theological Commission on 25 November 1981. On 15 February 1982 he resigned the pastoral governance of the Archdiocese of Munich and Freising. The Holy Father elevated him to the Order of Bishops assigning to him the Suburbicarian See of Velletri-Segni on 5 April 1993.

He was President of the Preparatory Commission for the Catechism of the Catholic Church, which after six years of work (1986-1992) presented the new Catechism to the Holy Father.

On 6 November 1998 the Holy Father approved the election of Cardinal Ratzinger as Vice-Dean of the College of Cardinals, submitted by the Cardinals of the Order of Bishops. On 30 November 2002 he approved his election as Dean; together with this office he was entrusted with the Suburbicarian See of Ostia.

In 1999 he was Special Papal Envoy for the Celebration of the XII Centenary of the foundation of the Diocese of Paderborn, Germany which took place on 3 January. Since 13 November 2000 he has been an Honorary Academic of the Pontifical

Academy of Sciences.

In the Roman Curia he has been a member of the Council of the Secretariat of State for Relations with States; of the Congregations for the Oriental Churches, for Divine Worship and the Discipline of the Sacraments, for Bishops, for the Evangelization of Peoples, for Catholic Education, for Clergy and for the Causes of the Saints; of the Pontifical Councils for Promoting Christian Unity, and for Culture; of the Supreme Tribunal of the Apostolic Signatura, and of the Pontifical Commissions for Latin America, "Ecclesia Dei", for the Authentic Interpretation of the Code of Canon Law, and for the Revision of the Code of Canon Law of the Oriental Churches.

Among his many publications special mention should be made of his "Introduction to Christianity", a compilation of University lectures on the Apostolic Creed published in 1968; "Dogma and Preaching" (1973) an anthology of essays, sermons and reflections dedicated to pastoral arguments.

His address to the Catholic Academy of Bavaria on "Why I am still in the Church" had a wide resonance; in it he stated with his usual clarity: "one can only be a Christian in the Church, not beside the Church".

His many publications are spread out over a number of years and constitute a point of reference for many people, especially for those interested in entering deeper into the study of theology. In 1985 he published his interview-book on the situation of the faith (The Ratzinger Report) and in 1996 "Salt of the Earth". On the occasion of his 70th birthday the volume "At the School of Truth" was published, containing articles by several authors on different aspects of his personality and production.

He has received numerous "Honoris Causa" Doctorates, in 1984 from the College of St. Thomas in St. Paul, Minnesota; in 1986 from the Catholic University of Lima; in 1987 from the Catholic University of Eichstätt; in 1988 from the Catholic University of Lublin; in 1998 from the University of Navarre; in 1999 from the LUMSA (Libera Università Maria Santissima Assunta) of Rome and in 2000 from the Faculty of Theology of the University of Wrocław in Poland.

Biography Copyright 2005 - Libreria Editrice Vaticana

Today we sit on the precipice of the prophecy's end. According to the prophecy, the current Pope may be the last Pope or he that ushers in the final figure. The Motto attributed to the sitting Pope is Gloria Olivæ ("Glory of the Olives") was inserted after Malachy's vision and the final Pope occurring after this one is Petrus Romanus (Peter the Roman) whose prophecy reads:

(In extreme persecution, the seat of the Holy Roman Church will be occupied by Peter the Roman, who will feed the sheep through many tribulations, at the term (end) of which the city of seven hills (Rome) will be destroyed, and the formidable Judge will judge his people.)

Could the current Pope be the deceiver waiting to reveal himself? When world turmoil arises will he change the church doctrine and present a false teaching in an attempt to bring other religions under his influence?

There are other prophecies spoken by prophets pertaining to and dovetailing with the prophecies of Malacy. These prophecies of cruel and turbulent times foretell natural disasters, persecution, comets, volcanoes, and battles in the world and in the church.

Shortly before his death in the 12th century St. Hildegard made a striking prophecy. It seems very applicable to the modern plague of tsunamis and earthquakes. The Pacific "ring of fire" has become active and hundreds of submerged volcanoes are becoming active again. His prophecy reads:

"The time is coming when princes and peoples will reject the authority of the Pope. Some countries will prefer their own Church rulers to the Pope. The German Empire will be divided. Before the comet comes, many nations, the good excepted, will be scourged by want and famine. The Great Nation in the ocean that is inhabited by people of different tribes and descent will be devastated by earthquake, storm, and tidal wave. It will be divided and, in great part, submerged. That nation will have many misfortunes at sea and lose it colonies. After the great comet, the Great Nation will be devastated by earthquakes, storms and great waves of water, causing much want and plagues. The ocean will also flood many other countries so that all coastal cities will live in fear, with many destroyed. All seacoast cities will be fearful, and many of them will be destroyed by tidal waves, and most living creatures will be killed, and even those who escape will die from a horrible disease. For in one of those cities does a person live according to the Laws of God. A powerful wind will rise in the North, carrying heavy fog and the densest dust, and it will fill their throats and eyes so that they will cease in their butchery and be stricken with great fear."

John of Vitiguerro, in the 13th century prophesied that "...The Pope will change his residence and the Church will not be defended for 25 months because during all that time there will be no Pope in Rome. After many tribulations, a Pope shall be elected out of those who survived the persecutions."

A 14th century bishop, John of the Cleft Rock prophesied that "...Towards the end of the world, tyrants and hostile mobs will rob the Church and the clergy of all their possessions and will afflict and martyr them. Those who heap the most abuse upon them will be held in high esteem. At that time, the Pope and his cardinals will have to flee Rome in tragic circumstances to a place where they will be unknown. The Pope will die a cruel death in his exile. The sufferings of the Church will be much greater than at any previous time in her history. But God will raise a holy Pope, and the Angels will rejoice."

Before he died in 1878, Pope Pius IX uttered these words: "There will come a great wonder, which will fill the world with astonishment. This wonder will be preceded by the triumph of revolution. The Church will suffer exceedingly. Her servants and chieftains will be mocked, scourged, and martyred." Prior to his prophecy, the Ecstatic of Tours uttered these prophetic words: "Before the war breaks out, food will become scarce and expensive. There will be little work for the workers, and fathers will hear their children crying for food. There will be earthquakes and signs in the sun. Toward the end, darkness will cover the Earth. When everyone believes that peace is ensured, when everyone least expects it, the Great Happening will begin."

A very old Italian prophecy, the author of which is lost to time, reads:

"When the White Pope and the Black Pope (Head of the Jesuits or an Anti-Pope) shall die during the same night, then there will dawn upon the Christian nations the Great White Day."

In the papal election, the cardinals gather together to vote by secret ballot. The cardinals choose three who collect the ballots, three who count the votes, and three who review the results. Two votes are taken every morning and two every afternoon until a two-thirds plus one majority is obtained. Catholic followers in St. Peter's Square watch the balloting by way of an ancient custom - the smoke rising from the palace chimney as the ballots are burned.

If the majority vote has not been reached, the smoke burns black. When the majority of ballots have chosen the next Pope, the chimney burns "white smoke" to signal the outcome of the election has been resolved.

There is a prophecy propagated within the church itself, which indicates there will be "five" Popes leading up to and including "the great Pope." The great Pope would be the first of the last three Popes who would follow in succession. The last Pope (the anti-Pope) will emerge at approximately the same time the anti-christ comes to power on the world scene.

According to some ancient prophetic texts, the papal time-line is very important because the final three Popes, including John Paul II, were to usher in the final age of the papal lineage of the Catholic church. According to the Paduan commentary, Pius XII (1939-1958) was the Pope chosen at the beginning of the anti-christ's reign.

This is obviously incorrect because Pope Pius XII doesn't fit the papal genealogical time-line. According to Catholic tradition, a Pope chosen to reign near the beginning of the anti-christ's rule would never be coronated. This Pope would be assassinated before he was crowned [or soon thereafter.] Pope Pius XII reigned for almost 19 years, and so he would have to be excluded in the count.

This could be the reason why one version of Malachy's prophecy skips the 111th Pope and jumps to the 112th - the 111th Pope never really gets the chance to reign as Pope. Also, Pius XII was the first of the five Popes in succession leading up to John Paul II (the 110th Pope). Pope John Paul II is the first of the last three Popes leading to the reign of the anti-christ. Although short-lived, the next elected Pope would follow in the traditions and work of Pope John Paul II. The succession of Popes may present a very interesting picture of the timing of world and end-time events; but where did the countdown begin?

As a parenthetical note, according to The Rosicrucian Fellowship's teaching about the Aquarian Age, the influences of the Age of

Aquarius began to be felt in 1969, signaling a shift in society. Aquarius has an intellectual influence which is original, inventive, mystic, scientific, altruistic, and religious. If we apply the biblical standard, "By their fruits ye shall know them," we would expect to see that the Aquarian Age would be ushered in by original endeavors along all lines connected with science, religion, mysticism, and altruism. The Aquarian Age will see the blending of religion and science to such a degree that a religious science and a scientific religion will be formed, each respecting and learning from the findings of the other, which will promote health, happiness, and enjoyment of life.

The Aquarian Age will bring with it an era of universal brotherhood, in preparation for which we see the barriers of race prejudice being broken all around us. To be sure, this is presently being accomplished under conditions of bloodshed and revolt. We can be certain, however, that although the sword, which had its reign during the Piscean Age, still is powerful, SCIENCE and ALTRUISM will rule during the Aquarian Age.

Since Aquarius is an airy, scientific, and intellectual sign, it is a forgone conclusion that the religion of that Age must be rooted in reason and able to solve the riddle of life and death in a manner that will satisfy both the mind and the religious instinct. In this respect, the Western Wisdom Teachings promulgated by the Rosicrucian Fellowship also are preparing the

31

way for the Aquarian Age by breaking down the fear of death engendered by the uncertainty surrounding the post-mortem existence. These Teachings show that life and consciousness continue under Laws as immutable as God, which tend to raise man to increasingly higher, nobler, and loftier states of spirituality. This shift was taking place during the papacy of Paul VI (the flower of flowers).

According to ancient prophecy and St. Malachy's papal time-line, we can provide a count down of the last five Popes before the Pope who will see the end. The count may began after Pope Pius XI which would make John Paul II the fifth, and the last great Pope, in the line of prophetic Popes.

110th Pope - John Paul II 1978-2005 (De Labore Solis – Labor of the sun) was born during a solar eclipse May 18, 1920 and died near a partial solar eclipse on April 8, 2005. The Pope of the eclipse was born when his mother was in labor during the eclipse. The sign is so plain that he may be the one designated as the true Pope. Pope John Paul II's funeral was held as the solar eclipse transpired on April 8th. – There is one version of St. Malachy omits De medietate Lunae (from half of the Moon).

It should be noted that in the Vatican there is a place where the portraits of all Popes are kept. After John Paul, the Vatican portrait gallery has a space for only two more papal portraits. This leaves room for John Paul II and Benedict XVI.

There is a prophecy that reads: "The Great Monarch and the Great Pope will precede Anti-Christ." [Wilson, 1883]

It will be the last great Pope that will reign just prior to the coming tribulation as Werdin d'Otrante (13 Century) wrote.

Is Benedict XVI Peter of Rome, or is he the one to usher him in? At first glance the last verse in the prophecy of Saint Malachy - "During the last persecution of the Holy Roman Church, there will sit upon the throne, Peter the Roman, who will feed the sheep amid great tribulations, and when these are passed, the City of the Seven Hills (Rome) will be utterly destroyed, and the awful Judge will then judge the people," could be read to mean that Peter the Roman will guide the church during the persecution, feeding the flock that remains.

There is, however, a great difference of opinion regarding this. The prophecy is read by some to mean that the real church will be persecuted and Peter the Roman (or Peter of Rome) will assume the seat of Saint Peter falsely, as a false Pope, and will serve his people, not God's people, even as God's people are persecuted.

St Hildegard (d.1179) wrote about a day of destruction that will come upon the entire world.
"A powerful wind will rise in the North carrying heavy fog and the densest dust (darkness) by divine command and it will fill their throats and eyes so they will cease their savagery and be stricken with a great fear..."

"Before the Comet comes, many nations, the good excepted, will be scourged with want and famine. The great nation [the United States] in the ocean that is inhabited by people of different tribes and descent by an earthquake, storm and tidal waves will be devastated."

"It will be divided, and in great part be submerged... The Comet by its tremendous pressure, will force much out of the ocean and flood many countries, causing much want and many plagues."

"All seacoast cities will be fearful and many of them will be destroyed by tidal waves, and most living creatures will be killed and even those who escape will die from a horrible disease. For in none of those cities does a person live according to the laws of God."

Pope John Paul II and The Secret of Fatima

The Third Secret is apocalyptic and therefore corresponds to the eschatological texts of Sacred Scripture. This is what Cardinal Ratzinger pointed out when he revealed that the Secret concerns the 'novissimi' - the 'last things' and corresponds to what is revealed in Sacred Scripture. Pope John Paul II, when asked about the Third Secret in Germany, stated:

"We must be prepared to undergo great trials in the not too distant future, trials that will require us to be ready to give up our lives..."

In 1976 Pope John Paul II, as Cardinal Karol Wojtyla, elaborated this theme during a visit to the United States saying:

"We are now standing in the face of the greatest historical confrontation humanity has gone through. I do not think that wide circles of the American Society or wide circles of the Christian Community realize this fully. We are now facing the final confrontation between the Church and the anti-Church, of the Gospel versus the anti-Gospel. It is a trial which the Church must take up."

In July 1916 an angel appeared at Fatima. There were three parts to the Secret of Fatima, which were revealed to three Portuguese children. The first two parts have long ago been revealed. These were concerning the appearance of the Angel at Fatima in 1916 and the Vision of Hell which Our Lady showed the children. The third part of the Secret was recently revealed.

The following reported dialogue of Pope John Paul II concerning the famous Third Secret of Fatima, the secret that was opened by Pope John XXIII in 1960 and which has not been fully and officially revealed by the Vatican, is very interesting. This Secret was revealed by Our Lady on July 13, 1917, to Lucia, Jacinta and Francisco. It was entrusted to Lucia to transmit it to the Holy Father. This she did by means of a letter, which was opened in 1960 as Our Lady indicated was to be done. It was this secret that the children, on August 13, 1917, would not reveal to the Masonic mayor of Ourem - even after being imprisoned and threatened with death.

The children would rather die than disobey Our Lady in this matter. But that it was to be eventually made public seems to be Lucia's understanding, because in the book by Father De Marchi, which Sister Lucia personally approved of, the author indicated that the Secret would be revealed by the Holy Father. Here is the confirmation, almost to the letter also, of the apocalyptic prophecy in the unofficial version of the 'Third Secret' which for years has been in circulation without being denied:

...the waters of the ocean will become vapor, and the foam will rise up overwhelming and drowning everything. Millions and millions of people will die hourly..."

Translation of the First and Second Parts of the Secrets of Fatima

This will entail my speaking about the secret, and thus answering the first question. What is the secret? It seems to me that I can reveal it, since I already have permission from Heaven to do so. God's representatives on earth have authorized me to do this several times and in various letters, one of which, I believe, is in your keeping. This letter is from Father José Bernardo Gonçalves, and in it he advises me to write to the Holy Father, suggesting, among other things, that I should reveal the secret. I did say something about it. But in order not to make my letter too long, since I was told to keep it short, I confined myself to the essentials, leaving it to God to provide another more favourable opportunity.

In my second account I have already described in detail the doubt which tormented me from 13 June until 13 July, and how it disappeared completely during the Apparition on that day.
Well, the secret is made up of three distinct parts, two of which I am now going to reveal.

The first part is the vision of hell.

Our Lady showed us a great sea of fire which seemed to be under the earth. Plunged in this fire were demons and souls in human form, like transparent burning embers, all blackened or burnished bronze, floating about in the conflagration, now raised into the air by the flames that issued from within themselves together with great clouds of smoke, now falling back on every side like sparks in a huge fire, without weight or equilibrium, and amid shrieks and groans of pain and despair, which horrified us and made us tremble with fear. The demons could be distinguished by their terrifying and repulsive likeness to frightful and unknown animals, all black and transparent. This vision lasted but an instant. How can we ever be grateful enough to our kind heavenly Mother, who had already prepared us by promising, in the first Apparition, to take us to heaven. Otherwise, I think we would have died of fear and terror.

We then looked up at Our Lady, who said to us so kindly and so sadly:

"You have seen hell where the souls of poor sinners go. To save them, God wishes to establish in the world devotion to my Immaculate Heart. If what I say to you is done, many souls will be saved and there will be peace. The war is going to end: but if people do not cease offending God, a worse one will break out during the Pontificate of Pius XI. When you see a night illumined by an unknown light, know that this is the great sign given you by God that he is about to punish the world for its crimes, by means of war, famine, and persecutions of the Church and of the Holy Father. To prevent this, I shall come to ask for the consecration of Russia to my Immaculate Heart, and the Communion of reparation on the First Saturdays. If my requests are heeded, Russia will be converted, and there will be peace; if not, she will spread her errors throughout the world, causing wars and persecutions of the Church. The good will be martyred; the Holy Father will have much to suffer; various nations will be annihilated. In the end, my Immaculate Heart will triumph. The Holy Father will consecrate Russia to me, and she shall be converted, and a period of peace will be granted to the world".[7]

Translation of the Third Part of the Secrets of Fatima

The third part of the secret revealed at the Cova da Iria-Fatima, on 13 July 1917.

I write in obedience to you, my God, who command me to do so through his Excellency the Bishop of Leiria and through your Most Holy Mother and mine.

After the two parts which I have already explained, at the left of Our Lady and a little above, we saw an Angel with a flaming sword in his left hand; flashing, it gave out flames that looked as though they would set the world on fire; but they died out in contact with the splendour that Our Lady radiated towards him from her right hand: pointing to the earth with his right hand, the Angel cried out in a loud voice: '<u>Penance</u>, <u>Penance</u>, <u>Penance</u>!'.

And we saw in an immense light that is God: 'something similar to how people appear in a mirror when they pass in front of it' a Bishop dressed in White 'we had the impression that it was the Holy Father'. Other Bishops, Priests, men and women, the religious ones going up a steep mountain, at the top of which there was a big Cross of rough-hewn trunks as of a cork-tree with the bark; before reaching there the Holy Father passed through a big city half in ruins and half trembling with halting step, afflicted with pain and sorrow, he prayed for the souls of the corpses he met on his way; having reached the top of the mountain, on his knees at the foot of the big Cross he was killed by a group of soldiers who fired bullets and arrows at him, and in the same way there died one after another the other Bishops, Priests, men and women. Religious, and various lay people of different ranks and positions. Beneath the two arms of the Cross there were two Angels each with a crystal aspersorium in his hand, in which they gathered up the blood of the Martyrs and with it sprinkled the souls that were making their way to God.

An interview with Maria Lucia for Clarification of the Meaning of the Secret

When asked, "Is the principal figure in the vision the Pope?", Sister Lucia replied at once that it was. She recalled that the three children were very sad about the suffering of the Pope, and that Jacinta kept saying: "Coitadinho do Santo Padre, tenho muita pena dos pecadores!" ("Poor Holy Father, I am very sad for sinners!"). Sister Lucia continued: "We did not know the name of the Pope; Our Lady did not tell us the name of the Pope; we did not know whether it was Benedict XV or Pius XII or Paul VI or John Paul II; but it was the Pope who was suffering and that made us suffer too".

As regards the passage about the Bishop dressed in white, that is, the Holy Father—as the children immediately realized during the "vision"—who is struck dead and falls to the ground, Sister Lucia was in full agreement with the Pope's claim that "it was a mother's hand that guided the bullet's path and in his throes the Pope halted at the threshold of death" (Pope John Paul II, Meditation from the Policlinico Gemelli to the Italian Bishops, 13 May 1994).

Before giving the sealed envelope containing the third part of the "secret" to the then Bishop of Leiria-Fatima, Sister Lucia wrote on the outside envelope that it could be opened only after 1960, either by the Patriarch of Lisbon or the Bishop of Leiria. Archbishop Bertone therefore asked: "Why only after 1960? Was it Our Lady who fixed that date?" Sister Lucia replied: "It was not Our Lady. I fixed the date because I had the intuition that before 1960 it would not be understood, but that only later would it be understood. Now it can be better understood. I wrote down what I saw; however it was not for me to interpret it, but for the Pope.

Summary of Malachy's Prophecies of The Last 10 Popes

1. The Burning Fire. PIUS X. 1903-1914. This Pope showed a burning passion for spiritual renewal in the Church.

2. Religion Laid Waste. BENEDICT XV. 1914-1922. Communism moved into Russia where religious life was laid waste. World War I brought the death of millions of Christians.

3. Unshaken Faith. PIUS XI. 1922-1939. Fascist powers in Germany and Italy. Communism and Fascism bloomed, which enraged Hitler.

4. An Angelic Shepherd. PIUS XII. 1939-1958. This Pope received visions which have not been made public. He was in the truest sense of the word an Angelic Pastor to the flock.

5. Pastor and Mariner. JOHN XXIII. 1958-1963. John was a pastor to the world, much beloved, and the Patriarch of Venice. The connection to "mariner" is made through his residence in the city.

6. Flower of Flowers. PAUL VI. 1963-1978. Paul's coat-of-arms depicts three fleurs-de-lis, corresponding to Malachay's prophecy. The English translation of "fleur-de-lis" (sometimes spelled "fleur-de-lys") is "flower of the lily." This symbol, depicting a stylized lily or lotus flower, has many meanings. Traditionally, it has been used to represent French royalty, and in that sense it is said to signify perfection, light, and life. Legend has it that an angel presented Clovis, the Merovingian king of the Franks, with a golden lily as a symbol of his purification upon his conversion to Christianity. Others claim that Clovis adopted the symbol when waterlilies showed him how to safely cross a river and thus succeed in battle.

7. Of the Half Moon. JOHN PAUL I. 1978-1978. John Paul I (1978-78) was born in the diocese of Belluno (beautiful moon) and was baptized Albino Luciani (white light). He became Pope on August 26, 1978, when the moon appeared exactly half

full. It was in its waning phase. He died the following month, soon after an eclipse of the moon.

8. The Labor of the Sun. JOHN PAUL II. 1978-2005. Pope John Paul II was the most traveled Pope in history. He survived an assassination attempt. He was born on May 18, 1920. On that date in the morning there was a near total eclipse of the sun over Europe. Prophecy - The 110th Pope is "De Labore Solis" (Of the Solar Eclipse, or, From the Toil of the Sun). Like the sun he came out of the East (Poland).

9. The Glory of the Olive. The 111th prophesy is "Gloria Olivae" (The Glory of the Olive). The Order of Saint Benedict has claimed that this Pope will come from their ranks and their order. The Order of Saint Benedict had a branch called The Olivetans. Thus, the name, Benedict XVI connects this Pope to the prophecy via the "Branch of the Olivetans" within the Benedictine order.

It is interesting that Jesus gave his apocalyptic prophecy about the end of time from the Mount of Olives.

This Pope will reign during the beginning of the tribulation Jesus spoke of. Saint Benedict himself prophesied that before the end of the world his Order, known also as the Olivetans, will triumphantly lead the Catholic Church in its fight

against evil. "The Order of St Benedict has claimed by tradition that this Pope will come from within the Order. St Benedict himself has prophesied that before the end of the world comes about, his Order will triumphantly lead the Catholic Church in its fight against evil. The Order of St Benedict is also known at the Olivetans..."
~ Peter Bander in 1973 (32 years <u>before</u> Pope Benedict XVI was elected Pontiff)

10. PETER THE ROMAN - This final Pope will likely be Satan, taking the form of a man named Peter who will gain a worldwide allegiance and adoration. He will be the final antichrist which prophecy students have long foretold. If it were possible, even the very elect would be deceived. The 112th prophesy states: "In the final persecution of the Holy Roman Church there will reign Petrus Romanus, who will feed his flock amid many tribulations; after which the seven-hilled city will be destroyed and the dreadful Judge will judge the people. The End."

Malachy is not alone in his prophecies. There is a long list of those who have warned of end times and the papacy.

Certain Catholic prophecies warn that a major "antipope" is to come—and since this has not happened—they could be interpreted to mean that the next Pope is likely to be an antipope:
Anna-Katarina Emmerick (19th century): I saw

again a new and odd-looking Church which they were trying to build. There was nothing holy about it... (Dupont, p. 116)

Yves Dupont {writer interpreting A. Emmerick}: They wanted to make a new Church, a Church of human manufacture, but God had other designs...The Holy Father shall have to leave Rome, and he shall die a cruel death. An anti-Pope shall be set up in Rome (Dupont, p. 116).

Jeanne le Royer (d. 1798): I see that when the Second Coming of Christ approaches a bad priest will do much harm to the Church (Culligan E. The Last World War and the End of Time. The book was blessed by Pope Paul VI, 1966. TAN Books, Rockford (IL), p. 128).

Catholic priest and writer R. Gerald Culleton (20th century): A schism of short duration is destined to break out...An antipope, of German origin, is to be set up, and finally Rome itself will be destroyed" (Culleton, p. 42).

Let us not forget that the present Pope, Benedict XVI is of German origin. Cardinal Joseph Ratzinger, Pope Benedict XVI, was born at Marktl am Inn, Diocese of Passau (Germany) on 16 April 1927.

Frederick William Faber (died 1863): Antichrist...Many believe in a demonical incarnation–this will not be so–but he will be utterly possessed...His doctrine an apparent contradiction of no religion, yet a new religion...He has an attending pontiff, so separating regal and prophetic office (Connor, Edward. Prophecy for Today. Imprimatur + A.J. Willinger, Bishop of Monterey-Fresno; Reprint: Tan Books and Publishers, Rockford (IL), 1984, p. 87).

Blessed Joachim (died 1202): Towards the end of the world Antichrist will overthrow the Pope and usurp his See (Connor, p. 76).

Merlin (7th century): There will come a German Anti-Pope. Italy and Germany will be sorely troubled. A French King will restore the true Pope (Culleton, p. 132).

St. Francis of Assisi (d. 1226): There will be an uncanonically elected Pope who will cause a great Schism, there will be divers thoughts preached which will cause many, even those in the different orders, to doubt, yea even agree with those heretics which will cause My order to divide, then will there be such universal dissentions and persecutions that if these days were not shortened even the elect would be lost (Culleton, p. 130).

Catholic writer and priest P. Huchedé (19th century): ...the false prophet...will not be a king, nor a general of an army, but a clever apostate, fallen from Episcopal dignity. From being an apostle of the Gospel he will become the first preacher of the false messiah...(Huchedé, P. Translated by JBD. History of Antichrist. Imprimatur Edward Charles Fabre, Bishop of Montreal. English edition 1884, Reprint 1976. TAN Books, Rockford (IL), p. 24).

Priest Herman Kramer (20th century): This false prophet possibly at the behest of Antichrist usurps the papal supremacy...His assumed spiritual authority and supremacy over the Church would make him resemble the Bishop of Rome...**He would be Pontifex Maximus, a title of pagan emperors, having spiritual and temporal authority**. Assuming authority without having it makes him the False Prophet...Though he poses as a lamb, his doctrines betray him.
(Kramer H.B. L. The Book of Destiny. Nihil Obstat: J.S. Considine, O.P., Censor Deputatus. Imprimatur: +Joseph M. Mueller, Bishop of Sioux City, Iowa, January 26, 1956. Reprint TAN Books, Rockford (IL), p. 319).

Prediction 2012- Dec 21, 2012 - Terence McKenna combines Mayan chronology with a New Age pseudoscience called "Novelty Theory" to conclude that the collision of an asteroid or some "trans-dimensional object" with the Earth, or alien contact, or a solar explosion, or the transformation of the Milky Way into a quasar, or some other "ultranovel" event will occur on this day.

Dec 23, 2012 The world to end, according to the ancient Mayan calendar. (Abanes p.342)

NASA has anxiety over 2012   2012 - NASA recently published a report detailing new magnetism on the Sun that will probably result in Major Solar Changes and destruction of satellite communications, GPS, Air Traffic, and Power Grids.

The report clearly states that a new Solar Cycle is possible resulting from a knot of magnetism that popped over the sun's eastern limb on Dec. 11th. 2007.

The report goes on to mention specific years which major Earthly impact will be seen. The exact quote which mentions these years states;
"Many forecasters believe Solar Cycle 24 will be big and intense. Peaking in 2011 or 2012, the cycle to come could have significant impacts on telecommunications, air traffic, power grids and GPS systems. (And don't forget the Northern Lights!) In this age of satellites and cell phones, the next solar cycle could make itself felt as never before."

"Both the Hopis and Mayans recognize that we are approaching the end of a World Age... In both cases, however, the Hopi and Mayan elders do not prophesy that everything will come to an end. Rather, this is a time of transition from one World Age into another. The message they give

concerns our making a choice of how we enter the future ahead. Our moving through with either resistance or acceptance will determine whether the transition will happen with cataclysmic changes or gradual peace and tranquility. The same theme can be found reflected in the prophecies of many other Native American visionaries from Black Elk to Sun Bear."
—   Joseph Robert Jochmans

Whether one reads the book of Revelation or one looks to the prophecy of Malachy, in both cases a man of evil is on the scene taking advantage of society in order to establish himself as a world leader. This man will be the Pope of the end times, an unholy person of great political or religious power, both manipulative and charismatic.

The Idea of unholy Popes is not a new one. Several despots have risen to the papacy through politics, power plays and bribes. The most infamous of these tarnished papacies and they came from the same family line.

The Borgia Popes

Two Spanish cousins, Domingo de Borya and Rodrigo de Borya, married and produced children that unite the line into what will become the Italian Borgias.

One of these children was Alfonso de Borya, who became Pope Callixtus III.

Callixtus III was the first Spanish Pope. He was seventy-seven years old when he assumed the throne of Saint Peter in 1455. His appointment was a compromise between factions that had become gridlocked. Both parties looked at him as a temporary solution until a more permanent solution. He was old for his time and had gout. It is assumed the parties making the decisions believed he would not last long. They were correct about the duration, but not about the influence. He ruled for only three years, but he was able to shoehorn two of his nephews into the position of cardinals, including a nephew who would be the zenith of infamy. Rodrigo, the son of his sister, became the second and last of the Spanish Popes. He was known as Alexander VI.

Alfonso de Borya had been the cardinal-priest in Valencia. In 1429,the Pope at the time, Pope Martin V, promoted him to Bishop of Valencia. Cardinal Alfonso had persuaded the French anti-Pope, Clement VIII, to submit to the authority of Martin, and Alfonso was duly rewarded for his services for helping to bring about the end of the Great Schism of the Catholic Church, where two Popes, one in France and one in Rome, ruled the Church.

Pope Callixtus organized a crusade to liberate Constantinople from the Turks. He funded his war

nothing that was not useful to himself. He had no care for justice, since in his days Rome was a den of thieves and murderers. Nevertheless, his sins meeting with no punishment in this world, he was to the last of his days most prosperous. In one word, he was more evil and more lucky than, perhaps, any other Pope for many ages before."
--- Francesco Guicciardini (as reported in Chamberlain)

There were holy and pious men who have sat upon the seat of Saint Peter, and there have been vicious animals that have risen to power within the church. Let us take a panoramic look at the Popes of old. Below is a list of Popes coming before Saint Malacy.

Popes before Malachy's Prophecies
The list below will also name significant anti-Popes, those who opposed the rightly elected Pope. These are not numbered.

1
St. Peter
(42-67)

2
St. Linus
(67-76)

3
St. Cletus
(76-88)

4
St. Clement I
(88-97)

5
St. Evaristus
(97-105)

6
St. Alexander I
(105-1l5)

7
St. Sixtus I
(1l5-125)

8
St.Telesphorus
(125-136)

9
St. Hyginus
(136-140)

10
St. Pius I
(140-155)

11
St. Anicetus
(155-166)

12
St. Soter
(166-175)

13
St. Eleutherius
(175-189)

14
St. Victor I
(189-199)

15
St. Zephyrin
(199-217)

16
St. Callistus

(217-222)

Callistus and the following three Popes were opposed by St. Hippolytus, antipope (217-236)

17
St. Urban I
(222-230)

18
St. Pontian
(230-235)

19
St. Anterus
(235-236)

20
St. Fabian
(236-250)

21
St. Cornelius
(251-253)
Opposed by Novatian, antipope (251)

22

St. Lucius I
(253-254)

23
St. Stephen I
(254-257)

24
St. Sixtus II
(257-258)

25
St. Dionysius
(256-268)

26
St. Felix I
(269-274)

27
St. Eutychianus
(275-283)

28
St. Caius
(283-296)

29
St. Marcellinus
(296-304)

The Holy See was vacant about 4 years.

30
St. Marcellus I
(308-309)

31
St. Eusebius
(309) (reigned for four months.)

32
St. Miltiades or Melchiades
(31l-314)

33
St. Sylvester I
(314-335)

34
St. Marcus
(336) (January 18 – October 7)

35
St. Julius I
(337-352)

36
Liberius
(352-366)
Opposed by Felix II, antipope (355-365)
antipope Felix II (355-365)

37
St. Damasus I
(366-384)
Opposed by Ursicinus, antipope (366-367)
antipope Ursicinus (366-384)

38
St. Siricius
(384-399)

"At a Roman council held by Pope Siricius in 386 an edict was passed forbidding priests and deacons to have conjugal intercourse with their wives...It may be said that by the time of St. Leo the Great (446) the law of celibacy was generally recognized in the West." – Catholic Encyclopedia,

39
St. Anastasius I
(399-401)

40
St. Innocent I
(401-417)

41
St. Zosimus
(417-418)

42
St. Boniface I
(418-422)
Opposed by Eulalius, antipope (418-419)
antipope Eulalius (418-419)

43
St. Celestine I
(422-432)

44
St. Sixtus III
(432-440)

45
St. Leo I
(440-461)

46
St. Hilarus
(461-468)

47
St. Simplicius
(468-483)

48
St. Felix III
(483-492)

49
St. Gelasius I
(492-496)

50
Anastasius II
(496-498)

51
St. Symmachus
(498-514)
Opposed by Laurentius, antipope (498-501)
antipope Laurentius (498-501-505)

52
St. Hormisdas
(514-523)

53
St. John I
(523-526)

54
St. Felix IV
(526-530)

antipope Diodorus (530)

55
Boniface II
(530-532)
Opposed by Dioscorus, antipope (530)

56
John II
(533-535)

57
Agapitus I
(535-536)

58
St. Silverius
(536-537)

59
Vigilius
(537.555)

60
Pelagius I
(556-561)

61
John III
(561-574)

62
Benedict I
(575-579)

63
Pelagius II
(579-590)

64

St. Gregory I
(590-604)

65
Sabinian
(604-606)

66
Boniface III
(607)

67
St. Boniface IV
(608-615)

68
Deusdedit or
St. Adeodatus
(615-618)

69
Boniface V
(619-625)

70
Honorius I
(625-638)

Holy See vacant 1 year and 6 months

71
Severinus
(640)

72
John IV
(640-642)

73
Theodore I
(642-649)

74
St. Martin I

75
St. Eugene I
(654-657)

76
St. Vitalian
(657-672)

77

Adeodatus II
(672-676)

78
Donus
(676-678)

79
St. Agatho
(678-681)

80
St. Leo II
(682-683)

81
St. Benedict II
(684-685)

82
John V
(685-686)

83
Conon
(686-687)

Theodore
(687)

Paschal
(687)

84
St. Sergius I
(687-701)

85
John VI
(701-705)

86
John VII
(705-707)

87
Sissinius
(708)

88
Constantine
(708-715)

89
St. Gregory II
(715-731)

90
St. Gregory III
(731-741)

91
St. Zacharias
(741-752)

92
Stephen II
(752)
Because he died before being consecrated, many authoritative lists omit him

93
Stephen III
(752-757)

94
St. Paul I
(757-767)

antipope Constantine (767)

antipope Philip (768)

95
Stephen IV
(767-772)
Opposed by Constantine II (767) and Philip (768),
antiPopes

96
Adrian I
(772-795)

97
St. Leo III
(795-816)

98
Stephen V
(816-817)

99
St. Paschal I
(817-824)

100
Eugene II
(824-827)

101
Valentine
(827)

102
Gregory IV
(827-844)

antipope John (844)

103
Sergius II
(844-847)

104
St. Leo IV
(847-855)
Opposed by John, antipope (855)

105
Benedict III
(855-858)
Opposed by Anastasius, antipope (855)

antipope Anastasius (855-880)

106
St. Nicholas
(858-867)

107
Hadrian II

108
John VIII
(872-882)

109
Marinus I
(882-884)

110
St. Hadrian III
(884-885)

111
Stephen V
(885-891)

112

Formosus
(891-896)

113
Boniface VI
(896)

114
Stephen VI
(896-897)

115
Romanus
(897)

116
Theodore II
(897)

117
John IX
(898-900)

118
Benedict IV
(900-903)

119
Leo V
(903)
Opposed by Christopher, antipope (903-904)
antipope Christopher (903-904)

120
Sergius III
(904-91l)

121
Anastasius III
(91l-913)

122
Lando
(913-914)

123
John X
(914-928)

124
Leo VI
(928)

125
Stephen VII
(928-931)

126
John XI
(931-935)

127
Leo VII
(936-939)

128
Stephen VIII
(939-942)

129
Marinus II
(942-946)

130
Agapitus II
(946-955)

131
John XII
(955-964)

142
John XVIII
(1004-1009)

143
Sergius IV
(1009-1012)

144
Benedict
VIII (1012-1024)
Opposed by Gregory, antipope (1012)
antipope Gregory (1012)

145
John XIX
(1024-1032)

146
Benedict IX
(1032-1044)
He appears on this list three separate times, because he was twice deposed and restored

147
Silvester III
(1045)
 Considered by some to be an antipope.

148
Benedict IX
(1045)

149
Gregory VI
(1045-1046)

150
Clement II
(1046-1047)

151
Benedict IX
(1047-1048)

152
Damasus II
(1048)

153
St. Leo IX
(1049-1054)

154

Victor II
(1055-1057)

155
Stephen IX
(1057-1058)

"Stephen X French Abbot of Monte Cassino, Benedict's monastery, becomes Pope and surrounds himself with leading "Reformers" per the Merovingian mandate to "Reform the Church" (meaning "Crush the Church" per the conspiracy)." – Merovingian Infiltration of the Christian World Through Monasticism.

antipope Benedict X (1058-1059)

156
Nicholas II
(1059-1061)
Opposed by Benedict X, antipope (1058).
Nicholas II, French from Burgundy becomes a leading reformer Pope.

157
Alexander II
(1061-1073)

Opposed by Honorius II, antipope (1061-1072)
antipope Honorius II (1061-1072)

158
St. Gregory VII
(1073-85)

"Gregory VII of Tuscany, part of the Carolingian kingdom of the Franks, and Cluniac monk becomes Pope and transforms the Church into a legal institution with a monarchial form of government. He seems not to have played his "expected role" as he came into conflict with the Holy Roman Emperor when he issued a general ban on lay investiture. He died exiled captive of the Normans."

Clement III
(1084-1100)

Guilbert - an antipope who opposed the following three Popes.

159
Bl. Victor III
(1086-1087)
"Victor III, Abbot of Monte Cassino, Benedict's monastery, becomes Pope."

160
Bl. Urban II
(1088-1099)

"Urban II was the French Prior of Cluny (Reformed Benedictines) and was of the "Eudes" family. The King of the Franks, Eudes, ruled from 888 to 898 and was considered one of the antecedent kings of the Capetian House of France. The royal lines entangle. The name of the Royal Capetian line of Burgundy, great grandson of Hugh Capet was Eudes I the Red of Burgundy who acceded 1079, nine years before Urban (Eudes) became Pope. Eudes the Red acceded in that specific year because his brother, Hugh I of Burgundy, had abdicated to become the Prior of Cluny. Both were sons of Henry of Burgundy who married Sibylle of Barcelona. Henry was son of Robert I of Burgundy, who was the son of Hugh Capet. Barcelona, home of their mother, was part of the Spanish March connected to Septimania and, here too, the Duke of Aquitaine in 1012 was Eudes of Aquitaine. Aquitaine and Septimania are significant:

It happens that Septimania (Languedoc) is the area where a Gnostic stronghold was and where the Jesus-Magdalene heresy took root. It was where there was a large population of Cathars, Gnostic Christians, who were given independent status by Pepin, Carolingian King. The Cathars were the last of the Gnostics to be killed en mass by soldiers sent in by the Pope Innocent III.

161
Paschal II
(1099-1118)

Opposed by Theodoric (1100), Aleric (1102) and Maginulf ("Sylvester IV", 1105-1111), antiPopes (1100).

"Certainly a religious Order of Canons of the Holy Sepulcher under the Rule of Saint Augustine was founded early in the twelfth century, and this Order soon established itself across Europe and acquired great wealth." – The Papal Orders

antipope Theodoric (1100-1102)

antipope Albert (1102)

antipope Sylvester IV
(1105-1111)

162
Gelasius II
(1118-1119)
Gregory VII
(1118-1121)
Opposed by Burdin ("Gregory VIII"), antipope (1118)

163
Callistus II
(1119-1124)
Opposed by Celestine II, antipope (1124)

This motto refers to Gherardo Caccianemici's surname. "Cacciare" means "to hunt",and "nemici" is the Italian word for "enemies". As his name foreshadowed,
Caccianemici would be driven from Rome by his own subjects.

169
Eugene III (1145-1153)
Motto: 3
1. Ex magnitudine montis
(Out of the greatness of the mountain)
2. Patria Ethruscus oppido Montis magni.
(Tuscan by nation, from the town of Montemagno. The motto refers to Pope Eugene's last name, "Montemagno.")
Hist.: Born in the castle of Grammont
 (latin: mons magnus), his family name was
 Montemagno

170
Anastasius IV (1153-1154)
Motto: 4
1. Abbas Suburranus
(Suburran abbot)
2. De familia Suburra.
(From the Suburra family.)

171
Adrian IV (1154-1159)

Motto: 5

1. De rure albo

(From the white countryside)

2. Vilis natus in oppido Sancti Albani.

(Humbly born in the town of St. Albans.)

Hist.: Born in the town of Saint-Alban. Educated at the St Albans School in Hertfordshire. Nicholas Breakspear was the bishop of Albano before becoming Pope.

Antipope

Victor IV (1159-1164)

Motto: 6

1. Ex tetro carcere

(Out of a loathsome prison.)

2. Fuit Cardinalis S. Nicolai in carcere Tulliano.

(He was a cardinal of St. Nicholas in the Tullian prison.) *Victor IV was a Ghibelline antipope supported by emperor Barbarossa and a minority of clergy and people in Rome. Most supported the man who would become Pope Alexander III. Victor belonged to a very powerful family and was able to secure a fair amount of support. When he died, Pachal III was named as his successor. There was a second antipope who went by the name of Victor IV. Cardinal Gregory Conti was elected as the successor to antipope Anacletus II in 1138. He, however, was, was convinced to submit to Innocent II through the efforts of Bernard of Clairvaux.*

Antipope

Paschal III (1164-1168)

Motto: 7

1. Via trans-Tiberina
(Road across the Tiber.)
2. Guido Cremensis Cardinalis S. Mariæ
Transtiberim.
(Guido of Crema, Cardinal of St. Mary across the
Tiber.)
As a cardinal, he had held the title of Santa Maria
in Trastevere.

Antipope
Callixtus III (1168-1178)
Motto: 8
1. De Pannonia Tusciæ
(From Tusculan Hungary)
2. Antipapa. Hungarus natione, Episcopus Card.
Tusculanus.
(Antipope. A Hungarian by birth, Cardinal Bishop
of Tusculum.)
He was John, Abbot of Struma, originally from
Hungary.

172
Alexander III (1159-1181)
Motto: 9
1. Ex ansere custode.
(Out of the guardian goose)
2. De familia Paparona.
(Of the Paparoni family.)
His family's coat of arms had a goose on it.

173
Lucius III (1181-1185)
Motto: 10
1. Lux in ostio.
(A light in the entrance)
2. Lucensis Card. Ostiensis.
(A Luccan Cardinal of Ostia.)
In 1159, he became Cardinal Bishop of Ostia. Lux may also be a wordplay on
Lucius.

174
Urban III (1185-1187)
Motto: 11
1. Sus in cribo
(Pig in a sieve)
2. Mediolanensis, familia cribella, quæ Suem pro armis gerit.
(A Milanese, of the Cribella (Crivelli) family, which bears a pig for arms. His family name Crivelli means "a sieve" in Italian.

175
Gregory VIII (1187)
Motto: 12
1. Enlis Laurentii
(The sword of St. Lawrence)
2. Card. S. Laurentii in Lucina, cuius insignia enses falcati.
(Cardinal of St. Lawrence in Lucina, of whom the arms were curved swords.)

He had been the Cardinal of St. Lawrence and his armorial bearing was a drawn sword.

176
Clement III (1187-1191)
Motto: 13
1. De schola exiet
(He will come from school)
2. Romanus, domo Scholari.
(A Roman, of the house of Scolari.)
His family name was Scolari.

177
Celestine III (1191-1198)
Motto: 14
1. De rure bouensi.
(From cattle country)
2. Familia Bouensi.
(Bovensis (Bobone) family.)
He was from the Bobone family; a wordplay on cattle (boves).

178
Innocent III (1198-1216)
Motto: 15
1. Comes signatus
(Designated Count)
2. Familia Comitum Signiæ.
(Family of the Counts of Signia [Segni])

Hist.: descendant of the noble Signy, later called Segni family

Pope Innocent III ordered the massacre of thousands of Gnostic Christians. The Cathars spent much of 1209 fending off the crusaders. The leader of the crusaders, Simon de Montfort, resorted to primitive psychological warfare. He ordered his troops to gouge out the eyes of 100 prisoners, cut off their noses and lips, then send them back to the towers led by a prisoner with one remaining eye. This only served to harden the resolve of the Cathars.

The army at Béziers attempted an attack but was quickly defeated, then pursued by the crusaders back through the gates and into the city. Arnaud, the Cistercian abbot-commander, is supposed to have been asked how to tell Cathars from Catholics. His reply, *"Caedite eos. Novit enim Dominus qui sunt eius."*—"Kill them all, the Lord will recognize His own." The doors of the church of St Mary Magdalene were broken down and the refugees dragged out and slaughtered. Reportedly, 7,000 people died there. Elsewhere in the town many more thousands were mutilated and killed. Prisoners were blinded, dragged behind horses, and used for target practice. What remained of the city was razed by fire. Arnaud wrote to Pope Innocent III saying: "Today your Holiness, twenty thousand heretics were put to the sword, regardless of rank, age, or sex."

179
Honorius III (1216-1227)
Motto: 16
1. Canonicus de latere
(Canon from the side)
2. Familia Sabella, Canonicus S. Ioannis Lateranensis.
(Savelli family, canon of St. John Lateran)
He was a canon for the church of Santa Maria Maggiore, and had served as papal
chamberlain in 1188.

180
Gregory IX (1227-1241)
Motto: 17
1. Auis Ostiensis.
(Bird of Ostia)
2. Familia Comitum Signiæ Episcopus Card. Ostiensis.
(Family of the Counts of Segni, Cardinal Bishop of Ostia.)
Hist.: before his election he was Cardinal of Ostia and the family coat of arms bear a bird on a gules background.

181
Celestine IV (1241)
Motto: 18
1. Leo Sabinus
(Sabine Lion)
2. Mediolanensis, cuius insignia Leo, Episcopus
Card. Sabinus
(A Milanese, whose coat of arms was a lion,
Cardinal Bishop of Sabina.)
He was Cardinal Bishop of Sabina and his
armorial bearing had a lion in it. Also
a play on words, referring to the Pope's last
name, Castiglioni.

182
Innocent IV (1243-1254)
Motto: 19
1. Comes Laurentius
(Count Lawrence)
2. domo flisca, Comes Lauaniæ, Cardinalis S.
Laurentii in Lucina.
(Of the house of Flisca (Fieschi), Count of
Lavagna, Cardinal of St. Lawrence in Lucina.)
He was the Cardinal-Priest of San Lorenzo in
Lucca, and his father was the Count
of Lavagna.

183
Alexander IV (1254-1261)
Motto: 20

1. Signum Ostiense
(Sign of Ostia)
2. De comitibus Signiæ, Episcopus Card. Ostiensis.
(Of the counts of Segni, Cardinal Bishop of Ostia.)
He was Cardinal Bishop of Ostia and member of the Conti-Segni family.

184
Urban IV (1261-1264)
Motto: 21
1. Hierusalem Campaniæ
(Jerusalem of Champagne)
2. Gallus, Trecensis in Campania, Patriarcha Hierusalem.
(A Frenchman, of Trecae (Troyes) in Champagne, Patriarch of Jerusalem.)
Hist.: native of Troyes, Champagne, later
 patriarch of Jerusalem

185
Clement IV (1265-1268)
Motto: 22
1. Draco depressus.
(Dragon pressed down)
2. cuius insignia Aquila vnguibus Draconem tenens.
(Whose badge is an eagle holding a dragon in his talons.)
His coat of arms had an eagle crushing a dragon.

186
Gregory X (1271-1276)
Motto: 23
1. Anguinus Uir
(Snaky man)
2. Mediolanensis, Familia vicecomitum, quæ angus pro insigni gerit.
(A Milanese, of the family of Viscounts (Visconti), which bears a snake for arms.)
The Visconti coat of arms had a large serpent devouring a male child feet first.

187
Innocent V (1276)
Motto: 24
1. Concionatur Gallus
(French Preacher)
2. Gallus, ordinis Prædicatorum.
(A Frenchman, of the Order of Preachers.)
He was born in south-eastern France and was a member of the order of Preachers.

188
Adrian V (1276)
Motto: 25
1. Bonus Comes
(Good Count/Companion)
2. Ottobonus familia Flisca ex comitibus Lauaniæ.
(Ottobono, of the Fieschi family, from the counts of Lavagna.)

He was a count and a wordplay on "good" can be made with his name, Ottobono (bono).

189
John XXI (1276-1277)
Motto: 26
1. Piscator Thuscus
(Tuscan Fisherman)
2. antea Ioannes Petrus Episcopus Card. Tusculanus.
(Formerly John Peter, Cardinal Bishop of Tusculum.)
John XXI had been the Cardinal Bishop of Tusculum.

190
Nicholas III (1277-1280)
Motto: 27
1. Rosa composita.
(Composite Rose)
2. Familia Vrsina, quæ rosam in insigni gerit, dictus compositus.
(Of the Ursina (Orsini) family, which bears a rose on its arms, called 'composite'.)
He bore a rose in his coat of arms.

191
Martin IV (1281-1285)
Motto: 28
1. Ex teloneo liliacei Martini

(From the tollhouse of lilied Martin)

2. cuius insignia lilia, canonicus, & thesaurarius S. Martini Turonen[sis].

(Whose arms were lilies. He was treasurer of St. Martin of Tours.)

He was Canon and Treasurer at the Church of St. Martin in Tours, France.

192

Honorius IV (1285-1287)

Motto: 29

1. Ex rosa leonine

(Out of the leonine rose)

2. Familia Sabella insignia rosa à leonibus gestata.

(Of the Sabella (Savelli) family, arms were a rose carried by lions.)

His coat of arms were emblazoned with two lions supporting a rose.

193

Nicholas IV (1288-1292)

Motto: 30

1. Picus inter escas.

(Woodpecker between food)

2. Picenus patria Esculanus

(A Picene by nation, of Asculum [Ascoli].)

He was from Ascoli, now called Ascoli Piceno, in Picene country.

194

St. Celestine V (1294)

Motto: 31

1. Ex eremo celsus.

(Elevated from a hermit)

2. Vocatus Petrus de morrone Eremita.

(Called Peter de Morrone, a hermit.)

Hist.: prior to his election he was a hermit
in the monastery of Pouilles. Also a play on words
(celsus/Coelestinus), referring to the Pope's chosen
name Celestine.

195

Boniface VIII (1294-1303)

Motto: 32

1. Ex undars benedictione.

(From the blessing of the waves)

2. Vocatus prius Benedictus, Caetanus, cuius insignia undæ.

(Previously called Benedict, of Gaeta, whose arms were waves.)

His coat of arms had a wave through it. Also a play on words, referring to the Pope's Christian name, "Benedetto."

196

Benedict XI (1303-1304)

Motto: 33

1. Concionator patereus

(Preacher From Patara)

2. qui uocabatur Frater Nicolaus, ordinis Prædicatorum.

(Who was called Brother Nicholas, of the order of Preachers.)

This Pope belonged to the Order of Preachers. Patara was the hometown of Saint Nicholas, a namesake of this Pope (born Nicholas Boccasini).

197

Clement V (1305-1314)

Motto: 34

1. De fessis aquitanicis.

(From the misfortunes/fesses of Aquitaine)

2. natione aquitanus, cuius insignia fessæ erant.

(An Aquitanian by birth, whose arms were fesses.)

He was a native of St. Bertrand de Comminges in Aquitaine, and eventually became Archbishop of Bordeaux, also in Aquitaine. His coat of arms displays three horizontal bars, known in heraldry as fesses.

198

John XXII (1316-1334)

Motto: 35

1. De sutore osseo.

(From a bony cobbler)

2. Gallus, familia Ossa, Sutoris filius.

(A Frenchman, of the Ossa family, son of a cobbler.)

1. Gallus Vicecomes
(French viscount)
2. nuncius Apostolicus ad Vicecomites
Mediolanenses.
(Apostolic nuncio to the Viscounts of Milan.)
He was born of a noble French family.

203
Gregory XI (1370-1378)
Motto: 41
1. Novus de uirgine forti
(New man from the strong virgin)
2. qui uocabatur Petrus Belfortis, Cardinalis S.
Mariæ nouæ.
(Who was called Peter Belfortis (Beaufort),
Cardinal of New St. Mary's.)
From the Beaufort family and Cardinal of Santa
Maria Nuova

Antipope
Clement VII (1378-1394)
Motto: 42
1. Decruce Apostolica.
(From the apostolic cross)
2. qui fuit Presbyter Cardinalis SS. XII. Apostolors
cuius insignia Crux.
(Who was Cardinal Priest of the Twelve Holy
Apostles, whose arms were a cross.)
His coat of arms showed a cross, quarterly
pierced.

Antipope
Benedict XIII (1394-1423)
Motto: 43
1. Luna Cosmedina.
(Cosmedine moon)
2. antea Petrus de Luna, Diaconus Cardinalis S. Mariæ in Cosmedin
(Formerly Peter de Luna, Cardinal Deacon of St. Mary in Cosmedin.)
He was the famous Peter de Luna, Cardinal of Santa Maria in Cosmedin.

Antipope
Clement VIII (1423-1429)
Motto: 44
1. Schisma Barchinonis.
(Schism of the Barcelonas)
2. Antipapa, qui fuit Canonicus Barchinonensis.
(Antipope, who was a canon of Barcelona.)

204
Urban VI (1378-1389)
Motto: 45
1. De inferno prægnãti.
(From a pregnant hell.)
2. Neapolitanus Pregnanus, natus in loco quæ dicitur Infernus.
(The Neapolitan Prignano, born in a place which is called Inferno.)

His family name was Prignano or Prignani, and he was native to a place called
Inferno near Naples.

205
Boniface IX (1389-1404)
Motto: 46
1. Cubus de mixtione
(Cube from a Mixture)
2. familia tomacella à Genua Liguriæ orta, cuius insignia Cubi.
(Of the Tomacelli family, born in Genoa in Liguria, whose arms were cubes.)
His coat of arms includes a bend checky — a wide stripe with a checkerboard
pattern.

206
Innocent VII (1404-1406)
Motto: 47
1. De meliore sydere.
(From a better star)
2. uocatus Cosmatus de melioratis Sulmonensis, cuius insignia sydus.
(Called Cosmato dei Migliorati of Sulmo, whose arms were a star.)
The prophecy is a play on words, "better" (melior) referring to the Pope's last name,
Migliorati (Meliorati). There is a shooting star on his coat of arms.

207
Gregory XII (1406-1415)
Motto: 48
1. Nauta de ponte nigro
(Sailor from a black bridge)
2. Venetus, commendatarius ecclesiæ Nigropontis.
(A Venetian, commendatary of the church of Negroponte.)
Was Bishop of Venice and the Bishop of Chalcice, Chalcice being located on the Isle of Negropont

Antipope
Alexander V (1409-1410)
Motto: 49
1. Flagellum Folis
(Whip of the Sun)
2. Græcus Archiepiscopus Mediolanensis, insignia Sol.
(A Greek, Archbishop of Milan, whose arms were a sun.)
His coat of arms had a large sun on it. Also, a play on words, referring to the Pope's last name, "Philarges."

Antipope
John XXIII (1410-1415)
Motto: 50
1. Ceruus Sirenæ

(Stag of the siren)

2. Diaconus Cardinalis S. Eustachii, qui cum ceruo depingitur, Bononiæ legatus, Neapolitanus.

(Cardinal Deacon of St. Eustace, who is depicted with a stag; legate of Bologna, a Neapolitan.)

Baldassarre Cossa was a cardinal with the title of St. Eustachius. St. Eustachius

converted to Christianity after he saw a stag with a cross between its horns.

Baldassarre's family was originally from Naples, which has the emblem of the siren.

208

Martin V (1417-1431)

Motto: 51

1. Corona ueli aurei

(Crown of the golden curtain)

2. familia colonna, Diaconus Cardinalis S. Georgii ad velum aureum.

(Of the Colonna family, Cardinal Deacon of St. George at the golden curtain.)

Oddone Colonna was the Cardinal Deacon of San Giorgio in Velabro. The word

"Velabrum" is here interpreted as derived from "velum aureum", or golden veil.

His coat of arms had a golden crown resting atop a column.

209

Eugene IV (1431-1447)

Motto: 52

1. Lupa cælestina

(Heavenly she-wolf)

2. Venetus, canonicus antea regularis Coelestinus, & Episcopus Senssis.

(A Venetian, formerly a regúlar Celestine canon, and Bishop of Siena.)

He belonged to the order of the Celestines and was the Bishop of Siena which bears a she-wolf on its arms.

Antipope

Felix V (1439-1449)

Motto: 53

1. Amator crucis

(Lover of the cross)

2. qui uocabatur Amadæus Dux Sabaudiæ, insignia Crux.

(Who was called Amadeus, Duke of Savoy, arms were a cross.)

He was previously the count of Savoy and therefore his coat of arms contained the cross of Savoy. Also, the prophecy is a play on words, referring to the antipope's

Christian name, "Amadeus."

210

Nicholas V (1447-1455)

Motto: 54

1. De modicitate lunæ

(From the meanness of Luna)

2. Lunensis de Sarzana, humilibus parentibus natus.

(A Lunese of Sarzana, born to humble parents.)

He was born in Sarzana in the diocese of Luni, the ancient name of which was Luna.

211

Callistus III (1455-1458)

Motto: 55

1. Bos pascens.

(Grazing ox)

2. Hispanus, cuius insignia Bos pascens.

(A Spaniard, whose arms were a pasturing ox.)

Hist.: Alphonse Borgia's arms sported a golden grazing ox. He had been secretary to Cardinal Domenico Capranica and Cardinal Albergatti before he was elected Pope

212

Pius II (1458-1464)

Motto: 56

1. De capra et Albergo

(From a nanny-goat and an inn)

2. Senensis, qui fuit à Secretis Cardinalibus Capranico & Albergato.

(A Sienese, who was secretary to Cardinals Capranicus and Albergatus.)

He had been secretary to Cardinal Domenico Capranica and Cardinal Albergatti before he was elected Pope.

213
Paul II (1464-1471)
Motto: 57
1. De ceruo et Leone
(From a stag and lion)
2. Venetus, qui fuit Commendatarius ecclesiæ
Ceruiensis, & Cardinalis tituli S. Marci.
(A Venetian, who was Commendatary of the
church of Cervia, and Cardinal of the title of St.
Mark.)
Possibly refers to his Bishopric of Cervia (punning
on cervus, "a stag") and his
Cardinal title of St. Mark (symbolized by a winged
lion).

214
Sixtus IV (1471-1484)
Motto: 58
1. Piscator minorita.
(Minorite fisherman)
2. Piscatoris filius, Franciscanus.
(Son of a fisherman, Franciscan.)
He was born the son of a fisherman and a
member of the Franciscans, also known as
"Minorites".

215
Innocent VIII (1484-1492)
Motto: 59
1. Præcursor Siciliæ

(Forerunner of Sicily)

2. qui uocabatur Ioãnes Baptista, & uixit in curia Alfonsi regis Siciliæ

(Who was called John Baptist, and lived in the court of Alfonso, king of Sicily.)

Giovanni Battista Cibò was named after John the Baptist, the precursor of Christ. In his early years, Giovanni served as the Bishop of Molfetta in Sicily.

216

Alexander VI (1492-1503)

Motto: 60

1. Bos Albanus in portu

(Bull of Alba in the harbor)

2. Episcopus Cardinalis Albanus & Portuensis, cuius insignia Bos.

(Cardinal Bishop of Albano and Porto, whose arms were a bull.)

In 1456, he was made a Cardinal and he held the titles of Cardinal Bishop of Albano and Porto. Also, Pope Alexander had a red bull on his coat of arms

217

Pius III (1503)

Motto: 61

1. De paruo homine

(From a small Man)

2. Senensis, familia piccolominea.

(A Sienese, of the Piccolomini family.)

His family name was Piccolomini, from piccolo "small" and uomo "man".

218
Julius II (1503-1513)
Motto: 62
1. Fructus Iouis iuuabit
(The fruit of Jupiter will help)
2. Ligur, eius insignia Quercus, Iouis arbor.
(A Genoese. His arms were an oak, Jupiter's tree.)
On his Coat of Arms was an oak tree, which was sacred to Jupiter. Pope Julius' family name, "Della Rovere," literally means "of the oak."

219
Leo X (1513-1521)
Motto: 63
1. De craticula Politiana
(From a Politian gridiron)
2. filius Laurentii medicei, & scholaris Angeli Politiani.
(Son of Lorenzo de' Medici, and student of Angelo Poliziano.)
His educator and mentor was the distinguished humanist and scholar, Angelo
Poliziano. The "Gridiron" is the motto evidently referring to St. Lawrence, who was martyred on a gridiron. This is a rather elliptical allusion to Lorenzo the Magnificent, who was Giovanni's father.

220
Adrian VI (1522-1523)
Motto: 64
1. Leo Florentius
(Florentian lion)
2. Florstii filius, eius insignia Leo.
(Son of Florentius, his arms were a lion.)
His coat of arms had two lions on it, and his name is sometimes given as Adriaan
Florens, or other variants, from his father's first name Florens (Florentius).

221
Clement VII (1523-1534)
Motto: 65
1. Flos pilæi ægri
(Flower of the sick man's pill)
2. Florentinus de domo medicea, eius insignia pila, & lilia.
(A Florentine of the Medicean house, his arms were pill-balls and lilies.)
The Medici coat of arms were emblazoned with six medical balls. One of these balls, the largest of the six, was emblazoned with the Florentine lily.

222
Paul III (1534-1549)
Motto: 66

1. Hiacinthus medicors.
(Hyacinth of the physicians)
2. Farnesius, qui lilia pro insignibus gestat, &
Card. fuit SS. Cosme, & Damiani.
(Farnese, who bore lilies for arms, and was
Cardinal of Saints Cosmas and Damian.)
Pope Paul's coat of arms were charged with six
hyacinths.

223
Julius III (1550-1555)
Motto: 67
1. De corona Montana
(From the Mountainous crown)
2. antea uocatus Ioannes Maria de monte.
(Formerly called Giovanni Maria of the Mountain
[de Monte])
His coat of arms showed mountains and palm
branches laid out in a pattern much like
a crown.

224
Marcellus II (1555)
Motto: 68
1. Frumentum flocidum
(Trifling grain)
2. cuius insignia ceruus & frumstum, ideo
floccidum, quod pauco tempore uixit in papatu.

(Whose arms were a stag and grain; 'trifling', because he lived only a short time as Pope.)
His coat of arms showed a stag and ears of wheat.

225
Paul IV (1555-1559)
Motto: 69
1. De fide Petri
(From Peter's faith)
2. antea uocatus Ioannes Petrus Caraffa.
(Formerly called John Peter Caraffa.)
He is said to have used his second Christian name Pietro.

226
Pius IV (1559-1565)
Motto: 70
1. Esculapii pharmacum
(Aesculapius' medicine)
2. antea dictus Io. Angelus Medices.
(Formerly called Giovanni Angelo Medici.)
His family name was Medici.

227
St. Pius V (1566-1572)
Motto: 71
1. Angelus nemorosus.
(Angel of the grove)
2. Michael uocatus, natus in oppido Boschi.

(Called Michael, born in the town of Bosco.)
He was born in Bosco, (Lombardy); the placename means grove. His name was
'Antonio Michele Ghisleri', and Michele relates to the archangel.

228
Gregory XIII (1572-1585)
Motto: 72
1. Medium corpus pilars.
(Half body of the balls)
2. cuius insignia medius Draco, Cardinalis creatus à Pio. IIII. qui pila in armis gestabat.
(Whose arms were a half-dragon; a Cardinal created by Pius IV who bore balls in his arms.)
The "balls" in the motto refer to Pope Pius IV, who had made Gregory a cardinal.
Pope Gregory had a dragon on his coat of arms with half a body.

229
Sixtus V (1585-1590)
Motto: 73
1. Axis in medietate signi.
(Axle in the midst of a sign.)
2. qui axem in medio Leonis in armis gestat.
(Who bears in his arms an axle in the middle of a lion.)
This is a rather straightforward description of the Pope's coat of arms.

230
Urban VII (1590)
Motto: 74
1. De rore coeli.
(From the dew of the sky)
2. qui fuit Archiepiscopus Rossanensis in Calabria, ubi mãna colligitur.
(Who was Archbishop of Rossano in Calabria, where manna is collected.)
He had been Archbishop of Rossano in Calabria where sap called "the dew of heaven" is gathered from trees.

231
Gregory XIV (1590-1591)
Motto: 75
1. De antiquitate Vrbis
(Of the antiquity of the city)
His father was a senator of the ancient city of Milan. The word "senator" is derived from the Latin word "senex", meaning old man.

232
Innocent IX (1591)
Motto: 76
1. Pia ciuitas in bello.
(Pious city in war)
He was the Patriarch of Jerusalem before succeeding to the Papacy.

233
Clement VIII (1592-1605)
Motto: 77
1. Crux Romulea
(Cross of Romulus)
He had been a cardinal with the title of Saint Pancratius. Saint
Pancratius was a Roman martyr.

234
Leo XI (1605)
Motto: 78
1. Vndosus uir.
(Wavy man)
He had been the Bishop of Palestrina. The ancient Romans attributed the origins of Palestrina to the seafaring hero Ulysses.
Also, he had only reigned for 27 days.

235
Paul V (1605-1621)
Motto: 79
1. Gens peruersa.
(Corrupted nation)
Pope Paul scandalized the Church when he appointed his nephew to the College of Cardinals. The word "nepotism" may have originated during the reign of this Pope.

236

Gregory XV (1621-1623)
Motto: 80
1. In tribulatione pacis
(In the trouble of peace)
His reign corresponded with the outbreak of the
Thirty Years War.

237
Urban VIII (1623-1644)
Motto: 81
1. Lilium et rosa.
(Lily and rose)
He was a native of Florence. Florence, in Italy,
has a red lily on its coat of arms.

238
Innocent X (1644-1655)
Motto: 82
1. Iucunditas crucis.
(Delight of the cross)
He was raised to the pontificate after a long and
difficult Conclave
on the Feast of the Exaltation of the Cross (off by
a day)

239
Alexander VII (1655-1667)
Motto: 83
1. Montium custos.
(Guard of the mountains)

His family arms include six hills with a star above them.

240
Clement IX (1667-1669)
Motto: 84
1. Sydus Olorum
(Constellation of swans)
Hist.: upon his election, he was apparently the occupant of the Chamber of Swans in the Vatican. The "star" in the legend refers to Pope Alexander VII, who had made Clement his personal secretary. The Italian word for swan, "Cigni," rhymes with Pope Alexander's last name, "Chigi."

241
Clement X (1670-1676)
Motto: 85
1. De flumine magno
(From a great river)
Pope Clement was a native of Rome.

242
Innocent XI (1676-1689)
Motto: 86
1. Bellua insatiabilis.
(Insatiable beast)
Pope Innocent had a lion on his coat of arms.

243
Alexander VIII (1689-1691)
Motto: 87
1. Poenitentia gloriosa.
(Glorious penitence)
His first name was "Pietro". The apostle Peter repented after he had denied his master three times.

244
Innocent XII (1691-1700)
Motto: 88
1. Rastrum in porta.
(Rake in the door)
His full name was Antonio Pignatelli del Rastrello. "Rastrello" in Italian means "rake."

245
Clement XI (1700-1721)
Motto: 89
1. Flores circundati.
(Surrounded flowers)
He had been a cardinal with the title of San Maria in Aquiro.

246
Innocent XIII (1721-1724)
Motto: 90
1. De bona Religione

(From good religion)
A play on words, referring to the Pope's chosen name, "Innocent." He was from the famous Conti family which had produced several Popes.

247
Benedict XIII (1724-1730)
Motto: 91
1. Miles in bello
(Soldier in War)
Pietro Francesco Orsini

248
Clement XII (1730-1740)
Motto: 92
1. Columna excelsa.
(Lofty column)
When still a cardinal, he had held the title of St. Peter in Chains. The name "Peter" is derived from the Greek word "petros," meaning "rock." Clement was a frustrated architect who ordered, and sometimes interfered with, the building of many churches. He
managed to salvage two columns of the Parthenon for his chapel at Mantua.

249
Benedict XIV (1740-1758)
Motto: 93
1. Animal rurale

(Country animal)

250
Clement XIII (1758-1769)
Motto: 94
1. Rosa Vmbriæ.
(Rose of Umbria)

251
Clement XIV (1769-1774)
Motto: 95
1. Vrsus uelox.
(Swift bear [later misprinted as Cursus velox Swift
Course or Visus velox SwiftGlance])
The Ganganelli family crest bore a running bear.

252
Pius VI (1775-1799)
Motto: 96
1. Peregrin apostolic
(Apostolic pilgrim)
Spent the last two years of his life in exile, a
prisoner of the French Revolution. To this point
his was the longest reign.

253
Pius VII (1800-1823)
Motto: 97
1. Aquila rapax

(Rapacious eagle)

254
Leo XII (1823-1829)
Motto: 98
1. Canis et coluber
(Dog and adder)
"Dog" and "snake" are common insults, and Leo was widely hated. The legend could be an allusion to the Pope's last name, Sermattei. "Serpente" is the Italian word for snake.

255
Pius VIII (1829-1830)
Motto: 99
1. Vir religiosus.
(Religious Man)
Another play on words, referring to the Pope's chosen name, "Pius".

256
Gregory XVI (1831-1846)
Motto: 100
1. De balneis hetruriæ
(From the baths of Etruria)
Hist.: prior to his election he was member of an order founded by Saint Romuald, at Balneo, in Etruria, present day Toscany. Pope Gregory XVI belonged to the Camaldolese order of monks.

The Camaldolese order is said to have begun with two monastic houses. The first of these houses was Campus Maldoli, and the second was Fonte Buono. "Fonte Buono" is Italian for "good fountain."

257
Pius IX (1846-1878)
Motto: 101
1. Crux de cruce
(Cross from cross)
Hist.:Pius XI was the last Pope to reign over the Papal States (the middle third of what is
 today Italy). He ended up being a prisoner of the Vatican, never venturing outside Vatican City.
A much heavier burden than his predecessors. During the pontificate of Pius IX, the House of Savoy, whose coat of arms is a white cross on a red background, reunited Italy and stripped the Pope of his territorial possessions. Pope Pius XII, commenting on the beatification process of Pius IX, used the words "per crucem ad lucem" (through the cross to light). Pius IX was finally beatified by Pope John Paul II in 2000.

258
Leo XIII (1878-1903)
Motto: 102
1. Lumen in cælo
(Light in the Heavens [sky])

Hist.: Leo XIII wrote encyclicals on Catholic social teaching that were still being digested
 100 years later. He added considerably to theology. His coat of arms had a shooting star.

259
St. Pius X (1903-1914)
Motto: 103
1. Ignis ardens
(Burning fire)
Hist.: The Pope had great personal piety and achieved a number of important reforms in
 the devotional and liturgical life of priests and laypeople. Pius advocated the codification of Canon law, daily communion and the use of Gregorian chant in the Catholic liturgy, and was an opponent of Modernism. He was the first Pope to be declared a saint in over 400 years, the previous one being Pope Pius V.

260
Benedict XV (1914-1922)
Motto: 104
1. Religio depopulata
(Religion laid waste)
Hist.: This Pope reigned during the Bolshevik Revolution in Russia, which strengthened the establishment of Communism. These years saw the worldwide spread of atheistic Communism.

261
Pius XI (1922-1939)
Motto: 105
1. Fides intrepida
(Intrepid faith)
Hist.: This Pope stood up to Fascist and
Communist forces lining up against him in the
lead up to World War II. Established Vatican City
as a country and the papacy as a head of state.

262
Pius XII (1939-1958)
Motto: 106
1. Pastor angelicus
(Angelic Shepherd)
Hist.: This Pope was very mystical, and is
believed to have received visions, some which
have yet to be fulfilled. People would kneel when
they received telephone calls from him. His
encyclicals add enormously to the understanding
of Catholic beliefs (even if they are now
overlooked because of focus on
the Second Vatican Council, which occurred so
soon after his reign).

263
John XXIII (1958-1963)
Motto: 107
1. Pastor et Nauta
(Shepherd and Sailor)
Hist.: Prior to his election he was patriarch of

Venice, a marine city, home of the gondolas.

264
Paul VI (1963-1978)
Motto: 108
1. Flos florum
(Flower of flowers)
Hist.: His arms displayed three lilies.

265
John Paul I (1978)
Motto: 109
1. De medietate Lunæ
(From the midst of the moon)
Hist.: Albino Luciani, born in Canale d'Agardo, diocese of Belluno, (beautiful moon) Elected Pope on August 26, his reign lasted about a month, from half a moon to the next half...His month-long reign began with the moon half-full.

266
John Paul II (1978-2005)
Motto: 110
1. De labore solis.
(Of the eclipse of the sun, or from the labor of the sun)
Hist.: Karol Wojtyla was born on May 18, 1920 during a solar eclipse. He also comes from behind the former Iron Curtain (the East, where the Sun rises).

He might also be seen to be the fruit of the intercession of the Woman Clothed with the Sun laboring in Revelation 12
(because of his devotion to the Virgin Mary).
His funeral occurred on 8 April, 2005 when there was a solar eclipse visible in the Americas.

267
Benedict XVI (2005-)
Motto: 111
1. Gloria oliuæ
(Glory of the olive.)
The Benedictine order traditionally said this Pope would come from their order, since a branch of the Benedictine order is called the Olivetans. St Benedict is said to have prophesied that before the end of the world, a member of his order would be Pope and would triumphantly lead the Church in its fight against evil.
While the Holy Father chose the name "Benedict", this does not seem enough to fulfill the prophecy.
Nor is it clear how Benedict XVI (a Bavarian) is "Glory of the Olives". Since he is said to have remarked in the Conclave after saying he would take the name Benedict that it was partly to honor Benedict XV, a Pope of peace and reconciliation, perhaps Benedict XVI will be a peacemaker in the Church or in the World, and thus carry the olive branch. Since this is an addition to Malachy's prophecy, is this the Pope who will actually fulfill the 112th prophecy, the actual final prophecy of Malachy?

Pope # 268 is either the Pope now in office, or he is yet to be chosen.

Motto: 112

In persecutione extrema S.R.E. sedebit Petrus Romanus, qui pascet oves in multis tribulationibus: quibus transactis civitas septicollis diruetur, & Judex tremêdus judicabit populum suum. Finis.

(In extreme persecution, the seat of the Holy Roman Church will be occupied by Peter the Roman, who will feed the sheep through many tribulations, at the term of which the city of seven hills will be destroyed, and the formidable Judge will judge his people. The End.)

Questions should be weighing on the minds of the rational person at this point. Do the Cardinals chose a Pope to fit the prophecies? Do the Popes, after being chosen, take steps to conform to the prophecies? Are we seeing or imposing patterns that are not there and simply looking for a coincidence tying Pope and prophecy? Are the prophecies real? How much circumstantial evidence must be compounded before the pattern of prophecy becomes clear or believable?

So many prophecies are converging. The Mayan

prophecy of the changing age, beginning December 21, 2012, the growing possibility of a solar flare strong enough to destroy the atmosphere, a comet or asteroid collision, a reversal of the earth's magnetic poles, global warming, earthquakes, volcanoes, tidal waves, or simply a man made nuclear or biological holocaust, from Malachy to Nostradamus, the voices of the prophets of old are crying out to be heard at this very moment.

Is Malachy's prophecy of tribulation and doom pointing to one of these scenarios?

At this very moment, Israel is planning a bombing raid on Iran to prevent them from completing assembly of a nuclear bomb. Israel knows that Iran will use such a device to destroy them. There is a great possibility that Israel's aggression will trigger a multinational war in the Middle East, which will spread throughout the world. Islam and Christianity may come into violent conflict around the globe.

What better opportunity will a false leader have to seize power than in the religious chaos ensuing from a war in which Israel and the Christian nations of the world are attacked by the Islamic nations?

Several prophecies mention objects falling from the heavens such as comets or asteroids. Some mention floods of such great dimensions that coastal cities will be swept away. These prophecies of comets, asteroids, and floods could easily go together. Famine and Plagues would follow closely on the heels of social disruption.

No one knows in what fashion the prophecy will be revealed. No one knows what catastrophe will arise, which will allow such a shift in political and religious power as to force the church to split and an anti-church to arise. In such times of world famine, disease and destruction mankind will be focused on survival while evil men take control.

This would be the dramatically perfect place to close this work, but there is one theological point that has reared its ugly head. If the last Prophecy states that Peter of Rome is the evil church ruler, the false prophet foretold in Revelation, it raises the question of the rapture. There is no rapture mentioned in Malachy's prophecy. It is a point so profound that if it were going to occur before the judgment that concludes the prophecy it would have been mentioned. In Malachy's day there was no concept of the rapture. The church simply looked forward to the return of the Lord, as Paul expected could occur even within his lifetime.

THE RAPTURE

The word "Rapture" is not found in the English Bible. The word comes from the Latin verb *rapere,* which means "to carry off, abduct, seize or take forcefully." To see the flavor of the word, compare the words "rape" or "raptor", which is a type of bird of prey such as a hawk. The word *rapere* was used in the Latin Vulgate of 405 A.D. to translate the phrase from Thessalonians 4:17, which is the primary biblical reference. The word, *"rapiemur"* "we shall be caught up" translating the Greek word *harpagÄ, which is the* passive mood, future tense of *harpazÅ*.

Although the doctrine of the resurrection of the dead was taught by Jesus in the Gospels and was an accepted belief common to all Christians, there was no thought, nor discussion in the area of eschatology about the 'Rapture' until the Reformation. Although Christians from the very beginning accepted, as scriptures clearly state, that, at some point the faithful would be "caught up" with Christ, it was always assumed this was a resurrection message. In modern eschatology the same scriptures are interpreted as the doctrine of the 'Rapture'. The Christian denominations that actually put eschatological emphasis on it are mostly those that appeared after the Reformation. The first known occurrence of a "rapture-like" theology or reference, which could be construed as a rapture doctrine, was that of Ephraem of Nisibis, in 373 A.D., who preached a sermon saying; "For all the saints and Elect of God are gathered, prior to the tribulation that is to come, and are taken to the Lord lest they see the confusion that is to overwhelm the world because of our sins."

The sermon was met with a thousand years of silence and the idea was rejected and ignored. The doctrine did not catch on enough to be repeated or even referenced as a consideration until it was re-visited in the Protestant Reformation and the rise of Dispensationalism.

Then in 1788 a precursor to the doctrine of the rapture appeared as an allusion. The story was written in a book penned in 1788 by a Catholic priest named Emmanuel Lacunza and published in Spain in 1812. The book spread, as did the intrigue of its storyline.

By combining verses and ideas from several books of the Bible, John Darby, a Brethren preacher, developed and taught the Rapture doctrine in 1827. Yes, the idea of the rapture, as set forth in most Protestant churches, has only been around since the early 1800's. This should give pause. It should cause us to ask if this is some new insight and revelation from God, or simply an idea derived from a combination of unrelated texts from various books of the Bible.

When relating texts from different books of the Bible we must always remember that we are reading separate books written at different times to various churches in differing areas for divergent purposes.

The evangelist, William Blackstone worked the idea into his book and popularized Rapture doctrine in his best seller, "Jesus is Coming." This was the "Left Behind" novel of its day. The idea of the rapture is a great read and makes for a heart stopping storyline. Popularity drove the idea from the novel into the pulpit.

In theological terms, the teaching of the rapture is a new doctrine. Its inception can be traced to an event in 1831 when Margaret McDonald, who claimed that God had shown it to her, first taught it, in Scotland. Chances are, she read it in the 1793 Blackstone novel, who probably heard of Derby's doctrine, who likely encountered the idea from Lacunza's audience.

The idea of the Rapture was slow to gain acceptance until it was promoted by John Nelson Darby, the founder of the Christian (Plymouth) Brethren movement. With the development of Fundamentalist Christianity around the turn of the 20th century, it was Cyrus Ignatius Scofield who became the champion of this new Rapture doctrine. The Rapture doctrine entered mainstream Christianity with its inclusion in the Scofield Reference Bible. There is no real history to the Rapture doctrine until the 1800's.

Since Christianity began, the texts used to justify the rapture theology were always regarded as 'resurrection' texts. Thus the earliest Creeds stated that Christ's return was the time when the Resurrection and Judgment Day would occur. The Nicene Creed reads; "He is seated at the right hand of God from whence He shall come to judge the quick and the dead".

The understanding of these texts is especially the case for 1Thessalonians 4:17 where the context is concern for the fate of those Christians who have already died. The text assures its readers that "the dead in Christ shall rise first" (1Thess. 4:16). "Rising" refers to rising from the dead and thus "resurrection" and not "rapture.

Other texts are as tenuous and weak at best especially when examined in the light of their context. For example, the expression "one shall be taken" in the Olivet Discourse of Matthew 24:40 references a flood first, signifying a disaster had occurred, and thus pointing to another disaster killing many people. For this reason as well as the historical timing of the verse, it has long been regarded by scholars as referring to the first century Roman catapult barrage of Jerusalem during the 42 month siege from A.D. 66 to A.D. 70 in which many people were randomly killed. This occurred after the time frame that Jesus would have given the speech, but during the time Matthew would have written the Gospel.

The verses used to define the rapture are vague in their timing and sequence, especially when added to those of the Book of Revelation. The indeterminate timeframe gave way to four distinct viewpoints. These are called, "pre-tribulation," mid-tribulation," "post-tribulation," and pre-wrath." (Also called pre-trib, mid-trib, post-trib.) Most would equate the category of mid-trib with that of

those who listened to them, over and over again. In the affairs of man we must ask the age old question, "Who is more foolish, the fool or those who follow him?" We will conclude by presenting an interesting, long, but partial list and history of end-time prophecies.

Here is a partial list of predictions, starting with the earliest known apocalyptic utterance. It was written in a terse, informational style using many sentence fragments; so if you are an O.C.D. English teacher, turn back now. The rest of us will enjoy the laugh. This list is taken from several Internet sources, which, in turn, document their sources. For more information please see: www.lifepositive.com, www.2think.org, www.abhota.info, www.religioustolerance.org, and other sites.

2800 BC - According to Isaac Asimov's Book of Facts (1979), an Assyrian clay tablet dating to approximately 2800 BC was unearthed bearing the words "Our earth is degenerate in these latter days. There are signs that the world is quickly coming to an end. Bribery and corruption are common." This is one of the earliest examples of moral decay in society being interpreted as a sign of the soon-coming end of days.

634 BC - Apocalyptic thinking gripped Romans, who feared the city would be destroyed in the 120th year of its founding. There was a myth that 12 eagles had revealed to Romulus a mystical

number representing the lifetime of Rome, and some early Romans hypothesized that each eagle represented 10 years. The Roman calendar was counted from the founding of Rome, 1 AUC (ab urbe condita) being 753 BC. Thus 120 AUC is 634 BC. (Thompson p.19)

389 BC – The first prophecy of Rome's destruction came and went. This caused some to figure that the mystical number revealed to Romulus represented the number of days in a year (the Great Year concept), so they expected Rome to be destroyed around 365 AUC (389 BC). (Thompson p.19)

1st Century - Jesus said, "Verily I say unto you, there be some standing here, which shall not taste of death, till they see the Son of Man coming in his kingdom." (Matthew 16:28) Apostles waited for His return until their death. Paul preached about the soon return of Jesus.

70 A.D. - The Essenes, a sect of Jewish ascetics with apocalyptic beliefs, may have seen the Jewish revolt against the Romans in 66-70 as the final end-time battle. (Source: PBS Frontline special Apocalypse!)

2nd Century - The Montanists believed that Christ would come again within their lifetimes and establish a new Jerusalem at Pepuza, in the land of Phrygia. Montanism was perhaps the first bona fide Christian doomsday cult. It was founded around 156 A.D. by the prophet Montanus and two followers, Priscilla and Maximilla. Even though Jesus did not return, the cult lasted for several centuries. Tertullian was the most famous follower of this sect. He is quoted as saying, "I believe it just because it is unbelievable." (Gould p.43-44)

247 A.D. - Rome celebrated its thousandth anniversary this year. At the same time, the Roman government dramatically increased its persecution of Christians. Christians came to believe that this was the End Of Days. (Source: PBS Frontline special Apocalypse!)

365 A.D. - Hilary of Poitiers predicted the world would end in 365. (Source: Ontario Consultants on Religious Tolerance)

380 A.D. - The Donatists, a North African Christian sect headed by Tyconius, looked forward to the world ending in 380. (Source: American Atheists)

Late 4th Century - St. Martin of Tours (316-397) wrote, "There is no doubt that the Antichrist has already been born. Firmly established already in his early years, he will, after reaching maturity, achieve supreme power." (Abanes p.119)

500 A.D. - Roman theologian Sextus Julius Africanus (160-240) claimed that the End would occur 6000 years after the Creation. He assumed

that there were 5531 years between the Creation and the Resurrection, and thus expected the Second Coming to take place no later than 500 A.D. (Kyle p.37, McIver #21)

500 A.D. - Hippolytus (died ca. 236), believing that Christ would return 6000 years after the Creation, anticipated the Parousia in 500 A.D. (Abanes p.283) Parousia is the return of Jesus to the earth.

500- A.D. The theologian Irenaeus, influenced by Hippolytus' writings, also saw 500 as the year of the Second Coming. (Abanes p.283, McIver #15)

793 A.D. - Apr 6, 793 - Spanish monk Beatus of Liébana prophesied the end of the world in the presence of a crowd of people, who became frightened, panicked, and fasted through the night until dawn. Hordonius, one of the fasters, was quoted as having remarked, "Let's eat and drink, so that if we die at least we'll be fed." This was described by Elipandus, bishop of Toledo. (Abanes p. 168-169, Weber p.50)

800 A.D. - Sextus Julius Africanus revised the date of Doomsday to 800 A.D. (Kyle p.37)

800 A.D. - Beatus of Liébana wrote in his Commentary on the Apocalypse, which he finished in 786, that there were only 14 years left until the end of the world. (Abanes p.168)

806 A.D. - Bishop Gregory of Tours calculated the End occurring between 799 and 806. (Weber p.48)

848 A.D. - The prophetess Thiota prophesied that the world would end this year. (Abanes p.337)

All dates shown here forward are A.D. unless otherwise noted.

970 - Mar 25, 970 – In Lotharingia, (a portion of the lands assigned to Emperor of the West, Lothair I,) theologians foresaw the end of the world on Friday, March 25, 970, when the Annunciation and Good Friday fell on the same day. They believed that it was on this day that Adam was created, Isaac was sacrificed, the Red Sea was parted, Jesus was conceived, and Jesus was crucified. Therefore, it followed that the end must occur on this day! (Source: Center for Millennial Studies)

992 - Bernard of Thuringia thought the end would come in 992. (Randi p.236)

995 – After the prophecy failed, seeing The Feast of the Annunciation and Good Friday also coincided in 992, some mystics conclude that the world would end within 3 years of that date, repeating the 970 prophecies. (Weber p.50-51)

1000 – Whenever a couple of zeros appear at the end of the date there will be apocalyptic thoughts.

There are many stories of paranoia around the year 1000. There are tales describing terror gripping Europe in the months before the date. There is disagreement about which stories are genuine since scholars claim ordinary people may not have even aware of what year it was. (See articles at "Center for Millennial Studies.") (Gould, Schwartz, Randi)

1033 - Jesus disappointed the Y-1-K crowd, so some irrepressible mystics re-thought the date, claiming there was a simple mistake. The return would occur at the thousandth anniversary of the Crucifixion, bringing the date to 1033. Burgundian monk Radulfus Glaber described a rash of millennial paranoia during the period from 1000-1033. (Kyle p.39, Abanes p.337, McIver #50)

1184 - Various Christian prophets foresaw the Antichrist coming in 1184. I do not know why. (Abanes p.338)

1186 – (Sep 23, 1186) - After calculating that a planetary alignment would occur in Libra on September 23, 1186 (Julian calendar), John of Toledo circulated a letter, known as the "Letter of Toledo", warning that the world was to going to be destroyed on this date, and that only a few people would survive. (Randi p.236)

1260 - Italian mystic Joachim of Fiore (1135-1202) determined that the Millennium would begin between 1200 and 1260. Where do these guys get their dates? (Kyle p.48)

1284 - Pope Innocent III expected the Second Coming to take place in 1284, 666 years after the rise of Islam. (Schwartz p.181)

1290 - The Joachites, who were followers of Joachim of Fiore, rescheduled the End of Time to 1290 when his 1260 prophecy failed. If at first you don't succeed, try, try again. (McIver #58)

1306 - In 1147 Gerard of Poehlde, believing that Christ's Millennium began when the emperor Constantine came to power, figured that Satan would become unbound at the end of the thousand-year period and destroy the Church. Since Constantine rose to power in 306, the end of the Millennium would be in 1306. (Source: Christian author Richard J. Foster)

1335 – The Joachites were still around, trying to figure things out. Their third prophecy of doomsday was 1335. Again, I have no idea why. (McIver #58) Joachites were very much preoccupied with the role of the Jews in prophecy and believed they had discovered the keys to understanding the timing of Bible prophecy.

1367 - Czech archdeacon, Militz of Kromeriz, claimed the Antichrist was alive and ready to march onto the stage of time. He would reveal himself between 1363 and 1367. The End would come between 1365 and 1367. Anti-psychotics were not invented yet. (McIver #67)

1370 - There is a thin line between visions and delusions. The proof is in the truth. Jean de Roquetaillade, a French ascetic foresaw the Millennium beginning in 1368 or 1370. The Antichrist was to come in the year 1366. (Weber p.55)

1378 - Arnold of Vilanova, a Joachite, wrote in his work "De Tempore Adventu Antichristi" that the Antichrist was to come in 1378. (McIver #62)

1420 - Feb 14, 1420 - Martinek Hausha, a Czech prophet, also known as Martin Huska was a member of the Taborite movement. He warned that the world would end in February 1420, February 14 at the latest. The Taborites rejected the corrupted church and insisted on biblical authority, not Papal authority. Even though Taborite theologians were versed in scholastic theology, they were among the first intellectuals to break free from centuries-old scholastic methods. (McIver #71, Shaw p.43)

1496 - The beginning of the Millennium, according to some 15th Century mystics. (Mann p. ix)

1504 - Italian artist Sandro Botticelli, a follower of Girolamo Savonarola, wrote a caption in Greek on his painting The Mystical Nativity: "I Sandro painted this picture at the end of the year 1500 in the troubles of Italy in the half time after the time according to the eleventh chapter of St. John in the second woe of the Apocalypse in the loosing of the devil for three and a half years. Then he will be chained in the 12th chapter and we shall see him trodden down as in this picture." He thought the Millennium would begin in three and a half years.. (Weber p.60)

1524 - Feb 1, 1524 - According to calculations of London astrologers made in the previous June, the end of the world would occur by a flood, (I thought God told us that would never happen again.), starting in London on February 1 (Julian). Around 20,000 people abandoned their homes, and a clergyman stockpiled food and water in a fortress he built. (Randi p.236-237)

1524 - Feb 20, 1524 - Astrologer Johannes Stoeffler saw the conjunction on a different day. The planetary alignment in Pisces, a water sign, was seen as the end of the Millennium, and the coming of the end by world flood. (Randi p.236-237)

1525 - Anabaptist Thomas Müntzer believed this date was the beginning of a new Millennium, and the "end of all ages." He led an unsuccessful peasants' revolt. The government disagreed with his prediction. He was arrested, tortured, and executed. (If he really thought it was the end of everything one wonders why a revolt would matter.) (Gould p.48)

1528 - Stoeffler's first attempt to predict the end of the world in 1524 failed. He then recalculated Doomsday to 1528. (Randi p.238) (Actually, up until today, all predictions have failed. The proof is that you are reading this.)

1528 - May 27, 1528   - Reformer Hans Hut predicted the end would occur on Pentecost (May 27, Julian calendar). (Weber p.67, Shaw p.44)

1532 - Frederick Nausea, a Viennese bishop, was certain that the world would end in 1532. He had heard reports of strange occurrences, including bloody crosses appearing in the sky alongside a comet. (I wonder if Mr. Nausea was sick when he got it wrong.) (Randi p. 238)

1533 - Anabaptist prophet Melchior Hoffman's prediction for the year of Christ's Second Coming, to take place in Strasbourg. He claimed that 144,000 people would be saved, while the rest of the world would be consumed by fire. (Kyle p.59) (We should note that usually wherever the prophet resides would be where the end begins. If a prophet predicts the end of time, normally only his followers are destined to make it out alive.)

1533 - Oct 19, 1533 -   Mathematician Michael Stifel calculated that the Day of Judgement would begin at 8:00am on this day. (McIver #88)

1534 - Apr 5, 1534 -   Jan Matthys predicted that the Apocalypse would take place on Easter Day (April 5, Julian calendar.) He went on to say only the city of Münster would be spared. (Shaw p.45, Abanes p.338) (He must have lived near the city.)

1537 - French astrologer Pierre Turrel announced four different possible dates for the end of the world, using four different calculation methods. The dates were 1537, 1544, 1801 and 1814. (Randi p. 239) He was playing the odds.

1544 - Pierre Turrel's doomsday calculation #2. (Randi p. 239)

1555 -   Around the year 1400, the French theologian Pierre d'Ailly wrote that 6845 years of human history had already passed. Using the "day as a thousand years" calculation. The "week of years theory places the 7th day or 7000 years at 1555. (McIver #72)

1556 - Jul 22, 1556 - A Swiss medical student, Felix Platter, writes about a rumor that on Magdalene's Day the world would end. (Weber p.68, p.249)

1583 - Apr 28, 1583 - Astrologer Richard Harvey predicts The Second Coming of Christ would take place at noon, on this day. A conjunction of Jupiter and Saturn would occur. Numerous astrologers in London had predicted the end.

(Skinner p.27, Weber p.93) (A conjunction is when two planets align, according to how they appear in the sky. They must appear within a few degrees of one another.)

1584 - Cyprian Leowitz, an astrologer, predicted the end would occur in 1584. (Randi p.239, McIver #105)

1588 - The end of the world according to the sage Johann Müller (Also known as Regiomontanus – Latin for King's Mountain). He was a mathematician and astrologer. (Randi p. 239)

1600 - Martin Luther believed that the End would occur no later than 1600. (Weber p.66)

1603 - Dominican monk Tomasso Campanella believed that the sun would collide with the Earth. (Weber p.83)

1623 - Eustachius Poyssel, a numerologist used his occult art to calculate 1623 as the year of the end of the world. (McIver #125)

1624 - Feb 1, 1624 - The same astrologers who predicted the deluge of February 1, 1524 recalculated the date to February 1, 1624 after their first prophecy failed. (Randi p.236-237) This way they would not have to be alive to endure another embarrassment.

1648 - Using the Kabbalah, a type of Hebrew numerology, Sabbatai Zevi, a rabbi from Smyrna, Turkey, predicted the Messiah's coming would be in 1648. There would be signs and miracles. People may have been excited, that is until he revealed that the Messiah would be Zevi himself. (Randi p.239, Festinger)

1654 – The sighting of a nova in 1572 brought physician Helisaeus Roeslin of Alsace, to claim the world would end in 1654 in a firestorm. (Randi p.240)

1657 - A group calling themselves "The Fifth Monarchy Men," predicted the apocalyptic battle and the overthrow of the Antichrist would take place between 1655 and 1657. They were what we would call a fundamentalist group who attempted to take over Parliament. They wanted to make the country a theocracy. The problem with theocracy is that the ruling party gets to determine what God's laws are. (Kyle p.67)

1658 - In his writings called, "The Book of Prophecies," Christopher Columbus claimed that the world was created in 5343BC, and would last 7000 years. Assuming no year zero, that means the end would come in 1658. Columbus was influenced by Pierre d'Ailly. (McIver #77)

1660 - Joseph Mede claimed that the Antichrist appeared way back in 456, and the end would come in 1660. This meant there was a 1204-year spread from start to finish. (McIver #147)

1666 – Many times there are no reasonable explanation of the dates reached by the prophets. In this case we can see the reasoning, although it is somewhat dubious. The date is 1000 (millennium) + 666 (number of the Beast). The date seems right because it followed a period of war in England. Londoners feared that 1666 would be the end of the world. Their fears were heightened by The Great Fire of London in 1666. (Schwartz p.87, Kyle p.67-68)

1666 - Rabi Sabbatai Zevi recalculated the coming of the Messiah to 1666. He was arrested for inciting public fear, and given the choice of converting to Islam or execution. He wisely elected to convert. (Festinger)

1673 - The prophecy of the group having failed the first time, Deacon William Aspinwall, a leader of the Fifth Monarchy movement, claimed the Millennium would begin by this year. (Abanes p.209, McIver #174)

1688 - John Napier, the mathematician who discovered logarithms, calculated this as the year of doom. (Weber p.92)

1689 - Pierre Jurieu, a Camisard prophet, predicted that Judgement Day would occur in

1736 - Cotton Mather's end-of-the-world prediction #3. This guy never stops. He is the energizer bunny of doomsday prophets. (Abanes p.338) (Remember – this guy was the witch burner. If anyone else had missed like this he would have torched them.)

1736 - Oct 13, 1736 - William Whitson predicted that London would meet its doom by flood on this day, prompting many Londoners to gather in boats on the Thames. (Randi) (Remember the rainbow, guys… God's promise not to drown the world…?)

1757 - In a vision, angels supposedly informed mystic Emanuel Swedenborg that the world would end in 1757. Few took him seriously. (Randi p.241, Weber p.104) Must have been those Swedish meatballs.

1761 - Apr 5, 1761 - William Bell claimed the world would be destroyed by earthquake on this day. There had been an earthquake on February 8 and another on March 8. He figured those were warnings. Kind of the one-two-three of earthquakes. The paranoia of Londoners gave way to anger and he was tossed into Bedlam, the London insane asylum that gave us that wonderful word. However, being that it was London, they did the deed in a very civilized manner. (Randi p.241)

1763 - Feb 28, 1763 - Methodist George Bell foresaw the end of the world on this date. (Weber p.102)

1780 - May 19, 1780   Smoke from large-scale forest fires to the west darkened New England skies for several hours. Being the nervous group that they were, the New Englanders believed that Judgement Day had arrived. (Abanes p.217)

1789 - Antichrist will reveal himself, according to 14th century Cardinal Pierre d'Ailly. (Weber p.59)

1790 - The Second Coming of Christ, according to Irishman Francis Dobbs. (Schwartz p.181)

1792 - The end of the world according to the Shakers. (Abanes p.338) The Shakers were originally located in England in 1747, in the home of Mother Ann Lee. The parent group was called the Quakers, which originated in the 17th century. Both groups believed that everybody could find God within him or herself, rather than through the organized church. Shakers tended to be more emotional in their worship. They are strict believers in celibacy, hence, their small numbers.

1794 - Charles Wesley, brother of Methodist Church founder John Wesley, predicted Doomsday would be in 1794. (Source: Ontario Consultants on Religious Tolerance)

1795 - English sailor Richard Brothers, calling himself "God's Almighty Nephew," predicted the Millennium would begin between 1793 and 1795. He expected the ten lost tribes of Israel would return. He also said God told him he would become king of England. He was shown the front door of the local insane asylum. (Kyle p.73, McIver #301)

1801 - Pierre Turrel's doomsday calculation - Strike three! The first one targeted 1537. (Randi p. 239)

1805 - Earthquake would wipe out the world in 1805, followed by an age of everlasting peace when God will be known by all. Presbyterian minister Christopher Love, was beheaded later. (Schwartz p.101)

1814   Pierre Turrel's doomsday calculation. Forth attempt... Please stop... just stop! The third attempt was in 1801. (Randi p. 239)

1814 - Dec 25, 1814 - This one is truly strange. A 64-year-old virgin prophet named Joanna Southcott claimed she would give birth to Jesus on Christmas Day. Witnesses claimed that she did appear pregnant. She died on Christmas Day. An autopsy proved that she was not pregnant. (Skinner p.109)

1820 - Oct 14, 1820 – Following on the heels of Southcott's death, a follower, John Turner, claimed the world would end. The prophecy failed and John Wroe took over leadership of the cult. (Randi p.241-242)

1836 - John Wesley, the founder of the Methodist, foresaw the Millennium beginning in 1836. He said the sign would be that the Beast of Revelation would rise from the sea. (McIver #269)

1843 - Harriet Livermore predicted Christ would return to the earth on this date. (McIver #699)

1843 - Apr 28, 1843 - Belief among William Miller's followers spawned gossip that the Second Coming would take place on this day. (Festinger p.16)

1843 - Dec 31, 1843 - Millerites expected Jesus to return at the end of 1843. (Festinger p.16)

1844 - Mar 21, 1844 - William Miller, leader of the Millerites, predicted Christ would return sometime between March 21, 1843 and March 21, 1844. He gathered a following of thousands of devotees. After the failed prophecy the cult experienced a crisis. They re-grouped and began reinterpreting the prophecy. This is more revisionist history of the church. (Gould p.49, Festinger p.16-17)

1844 - Oct 22, 1844 - Rev. Samuel S. Snow, an influential Millerite, predicted the Second Coming on this day. The date was soon accepted by Miller himself. On that day, the Millerites gathered on a hilltop to await the coming of Jesus. After the inevitable no-show, the event became known as the "Great Disappointment." It is said that Snow sold "ascension garments" to the waiting host and made a lot of cash on the deal. (Gould p.49, Festinger p.17)

1845 - The remaining members of Miller's cult, now called the Second Adventists, and the forerunners of the Seventh Day Adventists, claimed this would be the Second Coming. (Kyle p.91)

1846 – Obviously, the first time failed, so this is another Second Coming according to the Second Adventists. (Kyle p.91)

1847 - Harriet Livermore's Parousia prediction #2. (McIver #699)

1847 - Aug 7, 1847 "Father" George Rapp, founder of a sect known as the Harmonists (aka the Rappites,) established a commune in Economy, Pennsylvania. He was convinced that Jesus would return before his death. His speech on his deathbed was moving - "If I did not know that the dear Lord meant I should present you all to him, I should think my last moment's come." Rapp died before making the introduction. (Cohen p.23, Thompson p.283, Encyclopedia Britannica) (Thus, the first Rapp group began and ended.

1849 - Yet another Second Coming according to the Second Adventists. (Kyle p.91)

1851 -   AND, another Second Coming according to the Second Adventists. (Kyle p.91)

1856 - The Book of Revelation speaks of the King of the North invading Israel. The Crimean War in 1853-56 was seen by some as the Battle of Armageddon. Russia had planned to take control of Palestine from the Ottoman Empire. (McIver #437)

1862 - John Cumming of the Scottish National Church proclaimed the end of 6000 years since Creation. The world would end and the 1000 year reign of Jesus would begin. (Abanes p.283)

1863 - In 1823 Southcott, follower John Wroe, attempted and failed to walk on water. He then underwent a public circumcision. Many men may have been embarrassed. He then calculated that the Millennium would begin in 1863. (Skinner p.109)

1867 - The Anglican minister Michael Paget Baxter was an obsessive - compulsive date setter. Writer and philosopher, Charles Taylor, of the 19th century documented Baxter's follies as he predicted the End of the world. (McIver #348)

1868 - Michael Baxter claimed the Battle of Armageddon would take place this year. (Abanes p.338, McIver #349)

1869 – Baxter is back predicting another end. (McIver #350)

1870 - Jun 28, 1870 - France would fall, Jerusalem would be the center of the world, followed by Christ's millennial reign on Earth. This according to Irvin Moore's book "The Final Destiny of Man." (McIver #746)

1872 – Remember Baxter? He predicted another Armageddon in 1871-72 or thereabouts. (McIver #351)

1874 - The end of the world according to the Jehovah's Witnesses. This is the first in a long, long, long list of failed doomsday prophecies by this group. (Gould p.50, Kyle p.93)

1876 - The Parousia according to the newly formed Seventh Day Adventists, a group founded by former Millerites. (Abanes p.339)

1878 - You will lose count if you aren't careful. The end of the world according to the Jehovah's Witnesses. (Kyle p.93)

1880 - Thomas Rawson Birks in his book First Elements of Sacred Prophecy determined that the end of the world would be in 1880 by employing the time-honored Great Week theory. (McIver #371)

1881 – Redundant! The end of the world according to the Jehovah's Witnesses. (Kyle p.93)

1881 - The end of the world according to some pyramidologists, using the inch per year method. (Randi p.242)

1881 - 16th century prophetess Mother Shipton is said to have written the couplet:

The world to an end shall come
In eighteen hundred and eighty one.

In 1873, it was revealed that the couplet was a forgery by Charles Hindley, who published Mother Shipton's prophecies in 1862. People continued to buy and buy off on the book. (Schwartz p.122, Randi p.242-243)

1890 - Northern Paiute leader Wovoka predicted the Millennium. The prediction came from a trance he experienced during a solar eclipse in 1889. Wovoka was a practitioner of the Ghost Dance cult, a hybrid of apocalyptic Christianity and American Indian mysticism. (Gould p.56-57, p.69) As a note: Many spiritualists claim we all have American Indian guides in the spirit world. If one does the math it is immediately clear there aren't enough dead American Indians to go around.

163

1891 - In 1835 Joseph Smith, founder of Mormonism, foresaw the Second Coming taking place in 56 years' time, or about 1891. (Source: exmormon.org) As a side note, Smith also looked into a magic bag with stones in it to make his predictions. One such prediction was that the people of the moon were nice, conservative folk, who dressed in the Quaker fashion. (If someone these days were to stick his head into a bag and say things like this, he would be arrested for "huffing" glue.)

1895 - Reverend Robert Reid of Erie, Pennsylvania predicted and waited for The Millennium... and waited, and waited. (Weber p.176)

1896 – Baxter's back! Michael Baxter wrote a book entitled, "The End of This Age," in which he predicted the Rapture in 1896. According to Rev. Baxter, only 144,000 true Christians were to take the trip. (Thompson p.121) Recall that the rapture was not written about until the 1790's.

1899 - Charles A.L. Totten predicted that 1899 was a possible date for the end of the world. (McIver #924) Every day is a possible date.

1900 - Father Pierre Lachèze foresaw Doomsday occurring in
1900, eight years after the Temple in Jerusalem was to be rebuilt. (Weber p.136)

1900 - Followers of Brazilian ascetic Antonio Conselheiro expected the end to come by the year 1900. (Thompson p.125-126)

1900 - Nov 13, 1900   Over 100 members of the Russian cult Brothers and Sisters of the Red Death committed suicide, expecting the world to end on this day. (Sources: Portuguese article)

1901 – The sect of Catholic Apostolic Church claimed that Jesus would return by the time the last of its 12 founding members died. The last member died in 1901. (Boyer p.87)

1901 – Baxter's back. Rev. Michael Baxter foresaw the end of the world in 1901 in his book "The End of This Age: About the End of This Century." (Thompson p.121)

1908 – March 12, 1908 - Once again, it's Michael Baxter. In his book, "Future Wonders of Prophecy," he wrote that the Rapture was to take place on March 12, 1903 between 2pm and 3pm, and Armageddon was to take place on this day, which is after the Tribulation. One could argue the need to catch away the church after leaving it through the tribulations. (McIver #353)

1908 - Oct 1908 - Pennsylvanian grocery store owner Lee T. Spangler claimed that the world would meet a fiery end during this month.

Joseph Lumpkin

Possibly he planned to smoke some ribs. (Abanes p.339)

1910 - One of the many manic times for the J.W.'s. The end of the world according to the Jehovah's Witnesses. (Kyle p.93) This, of course, was followed by a period of depression and a dose of Prozac.

1910 - May 18, 1910 - The arrival of Halley's Comet would have many believing that cyanide gas from the comet's tail would poison the Earth's atmosphere. Con artists took advantage of people's fears by selling "comet pills" to make people immune to the toxins. There is a sucker born every minute. (Weber p.196-198, Abanes p.339)

1911 - 19th century Scottish astronomer and pyramidologist Charles Piazzi Smyth measured the Great Pyramid of Giza and converted inches to years, concluding that the Second Coming would occur between 1892 and 1911. (Cohen p.94)

1914 - Oct 1, 1914 – Yet another amazing prediction by The Jehovah's Witnesses. They viewed World War I as the Battle of Armageddon. (Skinner p.102)

1915 - The beginning of the Millennium according to John Chilembwe, fundamentalist leader of a rebellion in Nyasaland (present-day Malawi).

(Gould p.54-55, p.69) When the world didn't end he chose to force change.

1918 - The end of the world according to the Jehovah's Witnesses. For the sake of your herbivorous lions, please stop! (Kyle p.93)

1918 - Dec 17, 1919 - According to meteorologist Albert Porta, a conjunction of six planets on this date would cause a magnetic current to "pierce the sun, cause great explosions of flaming gas, and eventually engulf the Earth." Panic erupted in many countries around the world because of this prediction, and some even committed suicide. A similar prediction surfaced again in the 1970's regarding a planetary alignment in 1982. This was known as the Jupiter effect. (Abanes p.60-61)

1925 - The end of the world according to the Jehovah's Witnesses. You must be kidding! (Kyle p.93)

1925 - Feb 13, 1925 Margaret Rowan claimed the angel Gabriel appeared to her in a vision and told her that the world would end at midnight on this date, which was Friday the 13th. (Abanes p.45)

1928 - Spring 1928 - J.B. Dimbleby calculated that the Millennium would begin in the spring of 1928. The true end of the world, he claimed, wouldn't take pace until around the year 3000. (McIver #495)

1934 – The final battle was to begin in 1934 according to Chicago preacher Nathan Cohen Beskin, as he stated in 1931. (Abanes p.280)

1935 - Sep 1935 - In 1931, Wilbur Glen Voliva announced, "the world is going to go 'puff' and disappear in September, 1935." (Abanes p.287) Well... ok then.

1936 - Herbert W. Armstrong, founder of the Worldwide Church of God, told members of his church that the Rapture would take place in 1936. Only his true followers would be saved. After the prophecy failed, he changed the date three more times. I suppose this was one of the things that would later lead his son, Ted, to separate from the church and start his own cult. Later, Ted would love his secretary more than the church or his wife. (Shaw p.99)

1938 - Gus McKey wrote a pamphlet claiming the 6000th year since Creation would come between 1931 and 1938, signifying the end of the world. (Abanes p.283)

1941 - The end of the world according to the Jehovah's Witnesses. It just makes you angry after a while. (Shaw p.72)

1967 - Aug 20, 1967 - George Van Tassel, who claimed to have channeled an alien named Ashtar, proclaimed this time would be the beginning of the third woe of the Apocalypse, during which the southeastern US would be destroyed by a Soviet nuclear attack. (Alnor p.145) (And I thought that Ashtar was the other name for Chemosh, the Moabite god who demanded child sacrifice.)

1967 - Dec 25, 1967 - Danish cult leader Knud Weiking claimed that a being named Orthon was speaking to him, saying that there would be a nuclear war by Christmas 1967 that would disturb the Earth's orbit. His followers built a survival bunker in preparation for this catastrophe. Just as a note, if the earth's orbit is changed by only .5%, life as we know it would cease since temperatures would not support life. Bunkers would not work very well.

1969 - Aug 9, 1969 - Second Coming of Christ, according to George Williams, leader of the Morrisites, a 19th century branch of Mormonism. (Robbins p.77)

1969 - Nov 22, 1969 - The Day of Judgement, according to Robin McPherson, who supposedly channeled an alien named Ox-Ho. (Shaw p.154)

The 1960's must have brought out the lunatics. Everyone was channeling someone or some thing. Ever notice that no one channels Mr. Nobody?

1972 - Herbert W. Armstrong's Rapture prediction. (Shaw p.99) Armstrong pumped up his followers, telling them that only they know the truth and will go to heaven. Then he predicts the end so the flock would gather closer, be more devoted, and give more.

1973 - David Berg, also known as Moses David, leader of the Children of God, also known as the Family of Love, or just "The Family", predicted in his publication "The Endtime News" that the United States would be destroyed by the Comet Kohoutek in 1973. (McIver #2095)

1975 - The end of the world according to the Jehovah's Witnesses. (Kyle p.93) In this period of time I saw several J.W.'s that I knew run up huge credit card debt. When I asked about their reasoning I was informed the Witnesses were not worried about paying it back since they would not be here. I also pointed out that in the event they would be correct, the debts they left would force those left to pay higher rates. That seemed to be our problem, not theirs. Bankruptcies followed for many J.W.s.

1975 - Herbert W. Armstrong's Rapture prediction number 4. (Shaw p.99) It is amazing that these guys have followers, barring those with memory problems.

1975 - The Rapture, so said preacher Charles Taylor. This begins a compulsive streak of predictions for Mr. Taylor. (Abanes p.99)

1976 - Charles Taylor's Rapture prediction number 2. (Abanes p.99)

1977 - John Wroe (the Southcottian who had himself publicly circumcised in 1823) set 1977 as the date of Armageddon. (Randi p.243)

1977 - William Branham predicted that the Rapture would take place no later than 1977. Just before this, Los Angeles was to fall into the sea after an earthquake, the Vatican would achieve dictatorial powers over the world, and all of Christianity would become unified. (Babinski p.277) All those buying surfside homes in Arizona were disappointed.

1977 - Pyramidologist Adam Rutherford expected that the Millennium would begin in 1977. (Source: article by John Baskette)

1978 - In his book, "The Doomsday Globe," John Strong drew on scriptures, pyramidology, pole shift theory, young-earth creationism and other mysticism to conclude that Doomsday would come in 1978. (McIver #3237)

1980 - In his book, "Armageddon 198?", author, Stephen D. Swihart, predicted the End would occur sometime in the 1980s.

1980 - Charles Taylor's Rapture prediction number 3. (Abanes p.99)

1980 - Apr 1, 1980 - Radio preacher, Willie Day Smith, of Irving, Texas, claimed this would be the Second Coming. (Source: What About the Second Coming of Christ?)

1980 - Apr 29, 1980 - Leland Jensen, founder of the Bahá'ís "Under the Provisions of the Covenant", which is a small sect that mixes Bahá'í teachings with pyramidology and Bible prophecy, predicted that a nuclear holocaust would occur on this day, killing a third of the world's population. After the prophecy failed, Jensen rationalized that this date was merely the beginning of the Tribulation. (Robbins p.73)

1981 – Rev. Sun Myung Moon again announces the establishment of the Kingdom of Heaven. (Kyle p.148) I guess God didn't hear him the first time.

1981 - Charles Taylor's Rapture prediction number 4. (Abanes p.99)

1981 - Pastor Chuck Smith, founder of Calvary Chapel, wrote in his book "Future Survival," "I'm convinced that the Lord is coming for His Church before the end of 1981." Smith arrived at his calculation by adding 40 (one "Biblical generation") to 1948 (the year of Israel's statehood) and subtracting 7 for the Tribulation. (Abanes p.326) Way to go, Chuck!

1981 - June 28, 1981   - Rev. Bill Maupin, leader of a small Tuscon, AZ, sect named Lighthouse Gospel Tract Foundation, preached to his congregation, "rapture day was coming." Those who were saved would be "spirited aloft like helium balloons." Some 50 people gathered in a Millerite-like fashion. August 7, 1981. When his June 28 prediction failed, Bill Maupin claimed that doomsday would take place 40 days later. Maupin said that just as Noah's ark was gradually raised to safety over a period of 40 days, the same would happen to the world.
 (Source: Philosophy and the Scientific Method by Ronald C. Pine and Interviews with former members.) Have you ever noticed that the more words in a church's title the more wacked they can be?

1982 - Charles Taylor's Rapture prediction number 5. (Abanes p.99) Number five? Number five! GEEEZ!

1982 - Using the Jupiter Effect to support his thesis, Canadian prophet Doug Clark, claimed there would be earthquakes and fires that would kill millions. First, Jesus was to return and rapture

Christians away from the Tribulation (Abanes p.91)

1982 - Emil Gaverluk of the Southwest Radio Church suggested that the Jupiter Effect would pull Mars out of orbit and send it careening into the Earth. (Abanes p.100-101)

1982 - Mar 10, 1982 – The book, "The Jupiter Effect," by John Gribbin and Stephen Plagemann, stated that when the planets lined up, their combined_gravitational forces were supposed to bring the end of the world. The book sold well and the theory inspired several apocalyptic prophecies. (Abanes p.62)

1982 - Jun 25, 1982 – One of the most persistent and greatest hoaxes of the twentieth century is that of Maitreya and his prophet, Benjamin Crème. Crème is a British artist and founder of Tara Center. Over the years he predicted Maitreya's arrival on the world scene several times. He finally set a date of April 25, 1982. Of course once a date is set humiliation is not far behind. Supposedly Maitreya rung him up to tell him it just wasn't time yet.

Some history will help here. The Prophecy of Maitreya, stating that gods, men, and other beings will worship him implies that he is a teacher and a type of messiah. A quote from a Buddhist text reads,

" (all) will lose their doubts, and the torrents of their cravings will be cut off: free from all misery they will manage to cross the ocean of becoming; and, as a result of Maitreya's teachings, they will lead a holy life. No longer will they regard anything as their own, they will have no possession, no gold or silver, no home, no relatives! But they will lead the holy life of chastity under Maitreya's guidance. They will have torn the net of the passions, they will manage to enter into trances, and theirs will be an abundance of joy and happiness, for they will lead a holy life under Maitreya's guidance." (Trans. in Conze 1959:241)

Maitreya's coming is characterized by a number of physical events. The oceans are predicted to decrease in size, allowing Maitreya to cross them freely. Apparently this Messiah can't teleport or fly.

The event will also allow the unveiling of the "true" path of how to live. A new world will be built on these precepts. The coming ends a low point of human existence between the Gautama Buddah and Maitreya.

Crème's propaganda web page reads, "He has been expected for generations by all of the major religions. Christians know him as the Christ, and expect his imminent return. Jews await him as the Messiah; Hindus look for the coming of Krishna; Buddhists expect him as Maitreya Buddha; and Muslims anticipate the Imam Mahdi or Messiah."

Crème also took out an ad in the Los Angeles Times proclaiming "THE CHRIST IS NOW HERE", referring to the coming of Maitreya within 2 months. Crème supposedly received the messages from Maitreya through "channeling." (Grosso p.7, Oropeza p.155)

1982 - Fall 1982 - In the late '70s, Pat Robertson predicted the end of the world on a May, 1980 broadcast of the 700 Club. "I guarantee you by the end of 1982 there is going to be a judgment on the world," he said. (Boyer p.138)

1983 - Apocalyptic war between the U.S. and the Soviet Union, according to "The End Times News Digest." (Shaw p.182)

1983 - Charles Taylor's Rapture prediction number 6. (Abanes p.99)

1984 - Oct 2, 1984 - The end of the world according to the Jehovah's Witnesses. (Shermer p.203, Kyle p.91) You have got to love the unashamed, amazing chutzpah of these guys. The reasons they arrive at their dates show an amount of pure arrogance that is frightening. Since they believe that only 144,000 people will occupy heaven and since only members of their sect will make the cut, then when their membership reached 144,000 the rapture must occur. When that did not work, they reasoned that some were members but not true believers. Since money talks maybe the 144,000 will be made up of those who follow the rules and tithe. How ridiculous.

1985 - The end of the world according to Lester Sumrall in his book, "I Predict 1985." (Abanes p.99, 341)

1985 - Charles Taylor's Rapture prediction number 7. (Abanes p.99) It is time for a recap on Taylor. 1980 - Prophecy promoter Charles Taylor predicted the millennial reign of Christ to begin in 1995. He predicted the rapture would be in 1975, then in 1976, 1980, 1982, 1983, 1985, 1986, 1987, and, of course, 1989.

1985 - The Socialist National Aryan People's Party was convinced that Jesus would return in 1985. (Weber p.209) That's right, people. If you are white you can take the flight.

1985 - Mar 25, 1985 - The beginning of World War III, as prophesied by Vern Grimsley of the doomsday cult Family of God Foundation. This cult was a small offshoot of the Urantia Foundation, a loosely organized religious group that uses as its scripture a tedious 2000 page tome called the Urantia Book.

According to the on-line source, the Sceptic's Dictionary, "In short, the UB is over 2,000 pages of "revelations" from superhuman beings which "correct" the errors and omissions of the Bible. "Urantia" is the name these alleged superhumans gave to our planet. According to these supermortal beings, Earth is the 606th planet in Satania which is in Norlatiadek which is in Nebadon which is in Orvonton which revolves around Havona, all of which revolves around the center of infinity where God dwells. Others aren't so sure of the celestial origin of these writings. Matthew Block, for example, has identified hundreds of passages in the UB that are clearly based on human sources, but which are not given specific attribution. William Sadler, (the main author), admits on page 1343 that he used many human sources.

1987 - Charles Taylor's Rapture prediction number 8. (Abanes p.99) I thought about simply listing the prophecies from this guy in one line, but thought it better to place them in the time line simply for the humor.

1987 - Apr 29, 1987   Leland Jensen of the Bahá'ís "Under the Provisions of the Covenant" predicted that Halley's Comet would be pulled into Earth's orbit on April 29, 1986, and chunks of the comet would pelt the Earth for a year. The gravitational force of the comet would cause great earthquakes, and on April 29, 1987, the comet itself would crash into the Earth wreaking widespread destruction. When the prophecies failed, Jensen rationalized the failure as follows: "A spiritual stone hit the earth." (Robbins p.73, 78) What?

1987 Charles Taylor's Rapture prediction number 9. (Abanes p.99) One must wonder what Taylor thinks when he reads lists like this one and sees his name over and over, and over, and over, and....

1987 - Aug 17, 1987 - Everyone must visualize whirled peas. This is the year of the "Harmonic Convergence," bringing world peace. New Age author José Argüelles claimed that Armageddon would take place unless 144,000 people gathered in certain places in the world in order to "resonate in harmony" on this day. (McIver #2023, Kyle p.156, Wojcik p.207)

1988 – The reports of our death have been greatly exaggerated. Hal Lindsey's bestseller, "The Late, Great Planet Earth," calls for the Rapture in 1988, reasoning that it was 40 years (one Biblical generation) after Israel gained statehood. (Abanes p.85)

1988 - Charles Taylor's Rapture prediction number ten. (Abanes p.99)

1988 - Canadian prophet Doug Clark suggested 1988 as the date of the Rapture, in his book "Final Shockwaves to Armageddon." (Abanes p.91)

1988 - David Webber and Noah Hutchings of the Southwest Radio Church suggested that the Rapture would take place "possibly in 1987 or 1988." (Abanes p.101)

1988 - TV prophet J.R. Church (got to love this name for a preacher) in his book, "Hidden Prophecies in the Psalms," used a theory that each of the Psalms referred to a year in the 20th century. This would mean that Psalm 1 represents the events in 1901, and so on. Why the twentieth century was so special can only be due to the fact Mr. Church was living in it. The Battle of Armageddon would take place in 1994. (Abanes p. 103)

1988 - Colin Deal wrote a book entitled, "Christ Returns by 1988: 101 Reasons Why." (Oropeza p.175) There is one reason why not. It is because no one knows the day.

1988 - Sep 13, 1988 - Edgar C. Whisenant lightened the wallets of many a believer with his best-selling book, "88 Reasons Why The Rapture Will Be In 1988." He predicted the Rapture between September 11 and 13 (Rosh Hashanah). After Whisenant's prediction failed, he insisted that the Rapture would take place at 10:55 am on September 15.
After that prediction failed, he released another book: "The Final Shout: Rapture Report 1989." When that prediction failed, Whisenant pushed the date of the Rapture forward to October 3. (Kyle p.121, Abanes p.93, 94) I think they were written around the same time.

1989 - Charles Taylor's Rapture prediction number 11. (Abanes p.99) Are you keeping track of these, because, if this guy lives long enough, sooner or later he will get it right. The problem with end of day's prophecies is if you do get it right, there will be no one left to know it.

1989 - In his 1968 book, "Guide to Survival," Salem Kirban used Bishop Ussher's calculations to predict that 1989 would be the year of the Rapture. (Abanes p.283)

1989 - In 1978, Oklahoma City's Southwest Radio Church published a pamphlet entitled God's Timetable for the 1980s in which were listed prophecies for each year of the 1980s, culminating with Christ's return and the establishment of his kingdom on Earth in 1989. With the exception of a couple of predictable astronomical events, none of the predictions came true.

1990 -   Baptist preacher Peter Ruckman predicted that the Rapture would come round about the year 1990. (Source: article by Thomas Williamson)

1990 - The Jupiter Effect strikes again. Writer Kai Lok Chan, a Singaporean prophet, foresaw Jesus Christ returning sometime between 1986 and 1990. Armageddon (a war between the US and USSR) would take place between 1984 and 1988. He argued that the Jupiter Effect corroborated his claims. (McIver #2195)

1990 - Apr 23, 1990 - Elizabeth Clare Prophet, leader of the Church Universal and Triumphant, foresaw nuclear devastation and the end of most of the human race on this day, and convinced her followers to sell their property and move with her to a ranch in Montana. (Kyle p.156, Grosso p.7) In doing research, I have never heard such dribble as when I was instructed in her doctrine. According to E.C.P. Jesus is now a non-player. Michael has taken his place and is, of course, talking to her.

1991 - The Rapture, according to fundamentalist author Reginald Dunlop. (Shaw p.180)

1991 - Louis Farrakhan declared that the Gulf War would be the "War of Armageddon which is the final war." (Abanes p.307)

1991 - Mar 31, 1991 - An Australian cult looked forward to the Second Coming at 9:00 am on this day. They believed that Jesus would return through Sydney Harbour! (Source: Knowing the Day and the Hour)

1992 - Charles Taylor's Rapture prediction number 12. (Abanes p.99) Did I mention that he is the energizer bunny of Armageddon predictions?

1992 - Apr 26, 1992 - It was on April 26, 1989, Doug Clark announced on Trinity Broadcasting Network's show, " Praise the Lord," that World War III would begin within 3 years. (Abanes p.92) It was around this period of time I was employed at one of the TBN downlink transmitters as assistant engineer. Many times I received mail from little old ladies saying that they were giving their last few pennies on Earth to further the Kingdom of God. Pink hair dye, gaudy clothing, and jet fuel took most of it.

1992 - Apr 29, 1992 - When the LA riots broke out in response to the verdict of the Rodney King trial, members of the white-supremacist group Aryan Nations thought it was the final apocalyptic race war they had been waiting for. (20/20, NBC, Dec 12, 1999)

1992 - Sep 28, 1992 - Christian author Dorothy A. Miller in her book, "Watch & Be Ready! " predicted the "last trumpet" would sound on Rosh Hashanah, heralding the Second Coming. (McIver #2923)

1992 - "Rockin'" Rollen Stewart, a born-again Christian who made himself famous by holding up "John 3:16" signs at sporting events, thought the Rapture would take place on this day. Stewart went insane, setting off stink bombs in churches and bookstores and writing apocalyptic letters in a mission to make people get right with God. He is now serving a life sentence for kidnapping. (Adams p.18-20)

1992 - Oct 28, 1992 – The Hyoo-Go or Rapture movement was spreading through South Korea like a plague. Lee Jang Rim, leader of the Korean doomsday cult Mission for the Coming Days (also known as the Tami Church), predicted that the Rapture would occur on this date. Lee was convicted of fraud after the prophecy failed. (Thompson p.227-228, McIver #2747)

1993 - David Berg of the Children of God claimed in "The Endtime News!" that the Second Coming would take place in 1993. The Tribulation was to start in 1989. (McIver #2095, Kyle p.145)

1993 - Nov 14, 1993   - This was Judgment Day, according to self-proclaimed messiah Maria Devi Khrystos (A.K.A. Marina Tsvigun), leader of the cult Great White Brotherhood. (Alnor p.93)

1993 - Dec 9, 1993 - The United nations recognized Israel on May 15, 1949. James T. Harmon added 51.57 years to the date and subtracted 7 to arrive at the date of the Rapture, approximately December 9, 1993. He also suggested 1996, 2012 and 2022 as alternative rapture dates. So, we still have a chance at this one. (Oropeza p.89)

1994 - R.M. Riley, in his book "1994: The Year of Destiny," wrote that 1994 would be the year of the Rapture. (McIver #3098)

1994 - Charles Taylor's Rapture prediction number 13. (Abanes p.99) YAWN!

1994 - Om Saleem, an Arab Christian, prophesied that the Rapture would take place in 1994, after this the Antichrist was to reveal himself. (Oropeza p.148)

1994 - Dutch authors Aad Verbeek, Jan Westein and Pier Westein predicted the Second Coming in 1994 in their book, "Time for His Coming." (McIver #3348)

1994 - May 2, 1994 - Neal Chase of the Bahá'ís, "Under the Provisions of the Covenant," predicted that New York would be destroyed by a nuclear bomb on March 23, 1994, and the Battle of Armageddon would take place 40 days later. (Robbins p.79) It looks like everyone in the cult takes turns rolling dice to predict the end of time.

1994 - June 9, 1994 - Pastor John Hinkle claimed that God told him the Apocalypse would take place on this day. In a cataclysmic event, God was supposed to "rip the evil out of this world." When the prophecy failed, he claimed that it's only the beginning and it's taking place invisibly. (Oropeza p.167-168) I love invisible prophecies. I am wearing invisible pants right now.

1994 - Jul 25, 1994 - On July 19, 1993, Sister Marie Gabriel Paprocski announced to the world her prophecy that a comet would hit Jupiter on or before July 25, 1994, causing the "biggest cosmic explosion in the history of mankind" and bringing on the end of the world. Indeed, a comet did hit Jupiter on July 16, 1994. However, it is important to note that her announcement was made nearly two months after astronomer Brian Marsden

1997 - Mar 23, 1997 - Richard Michael Schiller predicted that an asteroid trailing behind Comet Hale-Bopp would bring destruction to the Earth on this date. As the date drew near he claimed the world would be destroyed 9 months later when the Earth supposedly would pass through the comet's tail.

1997 - Mar 26, 1997 - The infamous Heaven's Gate suicides occurred between March 24 and March 26, during a window of time predicted, a UFO trailing behind Comet Hale-Bopp would pick up their souls. Similarity between their prophecy and Schiller's one above are striking. The rumor of something following the comet started when amateur astronomer Chuck Shramek mistook a star for what he thought was a "Saturn-like object" following the comet. (Alnor p.13, 38)

1997 - Oct 1997 - The Rapture, according to Brother Kenneth Hagin.

1997 - Oct 23, 1997 - 6000th anniversary of Creation according to the calculations of 17th Century Irish Archbishop James Ussher. This date was a popular candidate for the end of the world. (Gould p.98)

1997 - Nov 27, 1997 - According to the Sacerdotal Knights of National Security, "A space alien captured at a UFO landing site in eastern Missouri cracked under interrogation by the CIA and admitted that an extraterrestrial army will attack Earth on November 27 with the express purpose of stripping our planet of every natural resource they can find a use for -- and making slaves of every man, woman and child in the world!" (Source: Ontario Consultants on Religious Tolerance)

1998 – According to Larry Wilson of "Wake Up America Seminars," the Second Coming would be around 1998. The Tribulation was supposed to start in 1994 or 1995, and during this period an asteroid was to hit the Earth. (Robbins p.220)

1998 - Centro, a religious cult in the Philippines, predicted that the end of the world would come in 1998. (Source: Ontario Consultants on Religious Tolerance)

1998 - The year of the Rapture, claimed Donald B. Orsden in his book, "The Holy Bible - The Final Testament": What is the Significance of 666?. "Take your super computers, you scientists, and feed the number 666 into them. The output will be the proof God gives that 1998 is the year Jesus will take the faithful with him...." (McIver #2986) During a period from 1999 and 2008 I worked as a system analyst on one of the fastest supercomputers in the U.S. The project was named, "Hypersonic Missile Technology." Out of the dozen or so rocket scientists there, none had the slightest idea of what he could possibly mean.

193

1998 - Henry R. Hall, author and nut case, predicts that the world will end in 1998 because, among other reasons, 666 + 666 + 666 = 1998. (McIver #2488)

1998 - Jan 8, 1998 – Thirty-one members of a splinter group of the Solar Temple cult headed by German psychologist Heide Fittkau-Garthe were convinced that the world would end at 8:00 pm on this day, but that the cult members' bodies would be picked up by a space ship. They were arrested by police on the Island of Tenerife, in the Canary Islands. The cultists were planning a mass suicide. (Hanna p.226 and FACTNet)

1998 - Mar 8, 1998 - All religions have their doomsday cults. One such cult is from Karnataka in southern India. They claimed that much of the world would be destroyed by earthquakes on this day, and the Indian subcontinent would break off and sink into the ocean. After the destruction, Lord Vishnu would appear on Earth. The leaders of the cult claimed that El Nino and the chaotic weather that accompanied it was a sign of the coming destruction.

1998 - Mar 31, 1998 - Hon-Ming Chen, leader of the Taiwanese cult God's Salvation Church, or Chen Tao - "The True Way" - claimed that God would come to Earth in a flying saucer at 10:00 am on this date. Moreover, God would have the same physical appearance as Chen himself. On March 25, God was to appear on Channel 18 on every TV set in the US. Chen chose to base his cult in Garland, Texas, because he thought it sounded like "God's Land." (Shermer p.204, McIver #2199)

1998 - May 31, 1998   - Author Marilyn J. Agee used convoluted Biblical calculations to predict the date of two separate Raptures. In her book "The End of the Age," she boldly proclaimed, "I expect Rapture I on Pentecost [May 31] in 1998 and Rapture II on the Feast of Trumpets [September 13] in 2007." (Agee)
When this failed she moved the date to Jun 7, 1998, then to Jun 14, 1998, then to Jun 21, 1998, and again on Sep 20, 1998, and May 22, 1999, and May 30, 1999, and June 20, 1999, and June 10, 2000, and Aug. 20, 2000 and May 28, 2001, and Nov 3, 2001, and Dec 19, 2001, and Jul 19, 2002, and Sep 13, 2007 (Oropeza p.89)

1998 - The Rapture, as per Tom Stewart's book 1998: Year of the Apocalypse. (McIver #3226)

1998 - Jun 6, 1998 - Eli Eshoh uses some numerical slight of hand to show that the Rapture was to take place in 1998. When nothing happened he claimed that it did indeed occur, but the number raptured was small enough not to be noticed. So... Eli was left behind?

1998 - Jul 5, 1998 - The Church of the SubGenius called themselves the only "One True Faith", (Don't they all?) designated this day X-Day. They expected the Xists from Planet X would arrive in flying saucers and destroy humanity on this day. Only ordained clergy who have paid their dues to the Church would be "ruptured" to safety! When that didn't come to pass, XX-Day was proclaimed to be July 5, 1999 and was declared the true end of the world. I can't wait until XXX-Day to see if they show up naked.

1998 - Sep 30, 1998 - Using Edgar Cayce's prophecies, Kirk Nelson predicted the return of Jesus on this date in his book "The Second Coming 1998."

1998 - Oct 10, 1998 - Monte Kim Miller, leader of the Denver charismatic cult "Concerned Christians", was convinced that the Apocalypse would occur on this date, with Denver the first city to be destroyed. The cult members mysteriously disappeared afterwards; but later resurfaced in Israel, where they were deported on suspicion of planning a terrorist attack at the end of 1999. Miller had also claimed he will die in the streets of Jerusalem in December 1999, to be resurrected three days later. (Sources: Watchman Fellowship, Ontario Consultants on Religious Tolerance)

1999 - Nov 1998 - The Second Coming and the beginning of the Tribulation, according to Ron Reese. He wrote that he had "overwhelming evidence" that this was true. (McIver #3081) He never showed anyone the evidence.

1999 - End of the world according to some Seventh Day Adventist literature. (Skinner p.105, Mann p.xiii) These mainline religions attempt to hide their mistakes from their followers. Most of their prophecies are never discussed with their believers.

1999 - End of the world according to the Jehovah's Witnesses. (Skinner p.102, Mann p.xiii) Speaking of hiding huge errors, the J.W.'s neglect to tell their followers that the church fathers were apocalyptic idiots.

1999 – It is astrologer Jeane Dixon again. She claimed the height of the Antichrist's power would be in 1999 when a terrible holocaust will occur, according to her book, "The Call to Glory." Dixon also claimed the Antichrist was born on Feb. 5, 1962. (Kyle p.153, Dixon p.168)

1999 - Edgar Cayce, The Sleeping Prophet, claimed a pole shift would cause natural disasters and World War III would begin. (Skinner p.127)

1999 - Linguist Charles Berlitz predicted the end of the world in his book, "Doomsday: 1999 A.D." (Kyle p.194)

1999 - Mar 25, 1999 - On September 25, 1997, Hal Lindsey predicted on his TV show, "International Intelligence Briefing," that Russia would invade Israel within 18 months. (Abanes p.286)

1999 - Apr 3, 1999 - The Rapture, according to H.J. Hoekstra. He believed we live on the inside of a hollow Earth. He used numerology to calculate the date of the Rapture.

1999 - May 8, 1999 - According to an astrological pamphlet circulating in India, the world was to meet its doom by a series of severe natural disasters on this date. This prediction caused many Indians to panic. (Source: BBC News)

1999 - Jun 30, 1999 - "Father" Charles L. Moore appeared on the Art Bell show November 26-27, 1998, claiming he knew the Third Secret of Fatima. According to Moore, the prophecy said that an asteroid would strike the Earth on June 30, bringing the End.

1999 - July 1999 - The_month made famous by 16th century soothsayer Nostradamus, the month that people have wondered about for over four centuries, is now at long last a part of history. (Source: The Mask of Nostradamus by James Randi): The Quatrain reads,
"L'an mil neuf cens nonante neuf sept mois
Du ciel viendra un grand Roy deffraieur
Resusciter le grand Roy d'Angolmois
Avant apres Mars regner par bon heur."

The year 1999, seven months,

From the sky will come a great King of Terror:
To bring back to life the great King of the Mongols,
Before and after Mars to reign by good luck.
(Quatrain X.72)

Between the time of Nostradamus and now the calendar changed. His seventh month, 13th day equates to August 13 of 1999. Both dates yielded nothing. According to Escape666.com, Nostradamus' King of Terror was to descend on Earth in September, heralding the beginning of the Tribulation and the Rapture. Escape666 said, regarding Nostradamus' infamous quatrain X.72: "now we know EXACTLY when he meant: SEPTEMBER 1999." However, as the end of September approached, they changed their date to October 12. They were embarrassed to try again.

1999 - Members of the Stella Maris Gnostic Church, a Colombian doomsday cult, went into Colombia's Sierra Nevada mountains over the weekend of July 3-4, 1999, weekend to be picked up by a UFO that would save them from the end of the world, which is to take place at the turn of the millennium. The cult members have disappeared. (Source: BBC News.)

1999 - Jul 5, 1999 – Remember X-day? Well, this is XX-day, according to the Church of the SubGenius. The Xists from Planet X and their saucers never came. Now all eyes are on XXX-day: July 5, 2000. Since it is XXX-day we assumed they will show up naked and have orgies.

1999 - Jul 7, 1999 - The Earth's axis was to shift a full 90 degrees at 7:00am GMT, resulting in a "water baptism" of the world, according to Eileen Lakes. (Get it? Baptism predicted by Lakes?) The site read,"
    7:00 a.m., on Wednesday, July 7, 1999
    at the World Greenwich Mean Time
    The earth will turn right by 90 degrees very instantly." Very instantly seems a little redundant, so we reported her writing to the Department of Redundancy Department.

1999 - Jul 28, 1999 - A lunar eclipse would signify the end of the Church Age and the beginning of the Tribulation, according to Gerald Vano. (Source: The Doomsday List.)

1999 - Aug 1999 - A cult calling itself Universal and Human Energy, also known as SHY (Spirituality, Humanity, Yoga), predicted the end of the world in August. (Source: FACTNet)

1999 - Aug 6, 1999 - The Branch Davidians believed that David Koresh would return to Earth on this day, 2300 days (Daniel 8:14) after his death. (Source: Ontario Consultants on Religious Tolerance)

1999 - Aug 11, 1999 - During the week between August 11 and August 18 a series of astronomical events took place: the last total solar eclipse of the millennium (Aug 11), the Grand Cross planetary formation (Aug 18), the Perseid meteor shower (Aug 12), the returning path of NASA's plutonium-bearing Cassini space probe's orbit (Aug 17-18), and Comet Lee's visit to the inner solar system. Add to this the fact that some of these events are taking place before the end of July according to the Julian calendar (See Nostradamus' prediction), and you have a recipe for rampant apocalyptic paranoia. Many alarmists were convinced that the Cassini space probe would crash into the Earth on August 18. The nuclear fuel it carried would poison a third of the world's population with its plutonium, fulfilling the prophecy of Revelation 8:11 concerning a star named Wormwood -- supposedly a metaphor for radiation poisoning ("Chernobylnik" is the Ukrainian word for a purple-stemmed subspecies of the wormwood plant). But as expected, Cassini passed by the Earth without a hitch.

1999 - Aug 14, 1999 - Escape666.com originally proclaimed on their website that a doomsday comet would hit Earth between August 11-14. (McIver #3362).

1999 - Aug 18, 1999 - The end of the world, as foreseen by Charles Criswell King, also known as "The Amazing Criswell." In his 1968 bestseller "Criswell Predicts:" "The world as we know it will cease to exist...on August 18, 1999.... And if you and I meet each other on the street that fateful day...and we chat about what we will do on the morrow, we will open our mouths to speak and no words will come out, for we have no future." August 18 happens to be Criswell's birthday. (Abanes p.43)

1999 - Aug 24, 1999 - In 1996, Valerie James wrote in The European Magazine, "The configuration of planets which predicted the coming of Christ will once again appear on Aug 24, 1999." (Ontario Consultants on Religious Tolerance)

1999 - Sep 1999 - The End, according to televangelist Jack Van Impe. (Shaw p.131)

1999 - Sep 3, 1999 - Judgment Day was to be on September 2 or 3, according to the notorious Japanese doomsday cult Aum Shinrikyo. Only members of Aum were to survive. These were the same people who gassed public transportation with sarin gas.

1999 - Sep 9, 1999 - 9/9/99 was to be the date when all older computers were to reset or crash due to their clocks running out of bits. Y2K would bring modern civilization to its knees. (Source: SF Gate)

1999 - Sep 11, 1999 - Bonnie Gaunt used the Bible Codes to prove that Rosh Hashanah 5760 (September 11, 1999) is the date of the Rapture.

1999 - Michael Rood also jumped on the Rosh Hashanah bandwagon. He claimed that this day is the first day of the Hebrew calendar year 6001, and after it failed, he changed the date to April 5, 2000. In reality, this day was the first day of 5760, but Michael claimed that there was a mistake in the calendar.

1999 - Sep 23, 1999 - Author Stefan Paulus combines Nostradamus, the Bible and astrology to arrive at September 23 as the date that a doomsday comet will impact the Earth. (Paulus p.57)

1999 - The Korean "Hyoo-go" movement spawned the Tami Sect. Proponents predict the demise of this earth in October 1999. (Source: Korea Times)

1999 - Jack Van Impe, your typical televangelist, having missed his last prediction just one month ago, predicted the Rapture and the Second Coming for October 1999. (Wojcik p.212)

1999 - Nov 7, 1999 - Internet doomsday prophet, Richard Hoagland, claimed that an "inside source" called him anonymously and warned of three objects that will strike the earth on this day.

The objects were supposedly seen during the August 11 eclipse.

1999 - Nov 29, 1999 - According to a vision he received in 1996, Dumitru Duduman claims that the destruction of America (i.e. Babylon) will occur around November 29, 1999.

1999 - Dec 21, 1999 - Sometime between November 23 and December 21, 1999, the War of Wars was to begin, claimed Nostradamus buff Henry C. Roberts. (Skeptical Inquirer, May/June 2000, p.6)

1999 - Dec 25, 1999 - The Second Coming of Christ, according to doomsday prophet Martin Hunter. (Oropeza p.57)

1999 - Dec 31, 1999 - Hon-Ming Chen's cult God's Salvation Church, now relocated to upstate New York, preached that a nuclear holocaust would destroy Europe and Asia sometime between October 1 and December 31, 1999. (Source: the Religious Movements Page)

2000 – It is true that each time the century mark rolls around people get edgy and make a lot of predictions. When it comes to those millennium markers people go a little crazy. The years 1000 and 2000 were favorites among prophets. Here as just a few of those predictions.

2000 - When his 1988 prediction failed, Hal Lindsey suggested the end might be in 2000, according to his recently published book, entitled "Planet Earth - 2000 A.D." (Lindsey p.306)

2000 - This is "The beginning of Christ's Millennium" according to some Mormon literature, such as the publication, "Watch and Be Ready: Preparing for the Second Coming of the Lord". The New Jerusalem will descend from the heavens in 2000, landing in Independence, Missouri. (McIver #3377, Skinner p.100) Like I said, the deed is always done where the prophet resides, because it is all about them.

2000 - 19th century mystic Madame Helena Petrova Blavatsky, the founder of Theosophy, foresaw the end of the world in 2000. (Shaw p.83)

2000 - In his book, "Observations upon the Prophecies of Daniel, and the Apocalypse of St. John", Sir Isaac Newton predicted that Christ's Millennium would begin in the year 2000 (Schwartz p.96)

2000 – Pop psychic, Ruth Montgomery predicted Earth's axis will shift and the Antichrist will reveal himself in 2000. (Kyle p.156, 195)

2000 - The establishment of the Kingdom of Heaven, according to Rev. Sun Myung Moon. (Kyle p.148)

2000 - A Vietnamese cult headed by Ca Van Lieng predicted an apocalyptic flood for 2000. But doomsday came much earlier for the cult members: he and his followers committed mass suicide in October 1993. (Source: Cult Observer archives)

2000 - End of Days will take place, say members of a Mormon-based cult near the Utah-Arizona border. Hundreds of members of the Fundamentalist Church of Jesus Christ of Latter-day Saints pulled their kids out of school in preparation for the Big Day. (Sep. 12, 2000 CNN article)

2000 - The Christian apocalyptic cult House of Prayer, headed by Brother David, expected Christ to descend onto the Mount of Olives in Jerusalem on this day. The Israeli government recently kicked them out of the country in a preemptive strike against their potential attempt to bring about the Apocalypse through terrorist acts such as blowing up the Dome of the Rock.

2000 - Bobby Bible, a 60-year-old fundamentalist, believed that Jesus would descend from Heaven at the stroke of midnight in Jerusalem and rapture his church.

2000 - A Philippine cult called Tunnels of Salvation taught that the world would end on January 1. The cult's guru, Cerferino Quinte, claimed that the world would be destroyed in an "all consuming rain of fire" on January 1. In order to survive the world's destruction, the cult members built an elaborate series of tunnels where he had stockpiled a year's worth of supplies for 700 people. (CESNUR)

2000 - UK native Ann Willem spent the New Year in Israel, expecting to be raptured by Jesus on New Year's Day. "It didn't happen the way it was supposed to," she said of the failure of the Rapture to take place. (USA Today p.5A, 1/3/00)

2000 - Jerry Falwell, a televangelist that some might mistake for a stand up comic is always a ray of sunshine and hope, which reminds me of Eeyore, foresaw God pouring out his judgment on the world on New Year's Day. According to Falwell, God "may be preparing to confound our language, to jam our communications, scatter our efforts, and judge us for our sin and rebellion against his lordship. We are hearing from many sources that January 1, 2000, will be a fateful day in the history of the world." (Christianity Today, Jan. 11, 1999)

2000 - Timothy LaHaye and Jerry Jenkins, authors of the bestselling Left Behind series of apocalyptic fiction, expected the Y2K bug to trigger global economic chaos, which the Antichrist would use to rise to power. (Source: Washington Post)

2000 - Jan 16, 2000 - Religious scholar Dr. Marion Derlette claimed the world is to end on January 16, according to an article in Weekly World News. This event is to occur after a series of natural and manmade catastrophes starting in 1997, and will be followed by an era of paradise on Earth. (This date is shown as January 6, 2000 in Richard Abanes' book "End-Time Visions." (Abanes p.43)

2000 - Feb 11, 2000 - On his broadcast on the morning of Feburary 7, 2000, televangelist Kenneth Copeland claimed that a group of scientists and scholars (he gave no specifics) studied the Bible in great detail and determined that Feb 11 would be the last day of the 6000th year since Creation, a date when the Apocalypse would presumably happen. Copeland did not imply he believed this to be accurate, though, but he went on to say that the Rapture will come soon. (Has anyone ever seen Copeland smile? So much for the joy of the Lord being our strength.)

2000 - Mar 2000 - The Rapture is to take place in March 2000, 3 1/2 years after Christ's Second Coming, according to Marvin Byers. (Oropeza p.29)

2000 - Apr 6, 2000 - The Second Coming of Christ according to James Harmston of the Mormon sect, "True and Living Church of Jesus

Christ of Saints of The Last Days". (As opposed to the false death church?) (McIver #2496)

2000 - Apr 2000 - The Whites, a family of ascetic doomsday cultists living near Jerusalem, expected the End to take place in March or April after the Ark of the Covenant was to reappear in a cave in the Old City in Jerusalem. They claimed that there was a mistake in the chronology of the Hebrew calendar and that the year 6001 will begin this Spring. In reality, Sep. 11, 1999 to Sep. 30, 2000 is the Hebrew year 5760. This means that the Hebrew year 6000 is 2240 A.D.

2000 - May 5, 2000 - According to archaeologist Richard W. Noone in his book, "5/5/2000 Ice: The Ultimate Disaster", a buildup of excess ice in Antarctica is causing the earth to become precariously unbalanced. All that's needed to upset this supposed imbalance and cause the pole shift, which would cause billions of tons of ice to go cascading across the continents. Where did this fool get his degree.

2000 - The Nuwaubians, also known as the Holy Tabernacle Ministries or Ancient Mystical Order of Melchizedek, claimed that the planetary lineup would cause a "star holocaust," pulling the planets toward the sun. (Alnor p.121)

2000 - May 9, 2000 - Toshio Hiji, having analyzed the quatrains of Nostradamus, announced that the Giant Deluge of Noah would inundate the

2001 -Sep 11, 2001 - Not a single prophet, soothsayer, or fortuneteller saw what was coming. The World Trade Center was destroyed and the Pentagon attacked by madmen, causing thousands of deaths. This should prove beyond a doubt that the future is God's alone. Although, I must say that the Nostradamus followers have a gift for taking his vague prophecies and twisting them to fit past events. Funny, they never foretell future happenings. The same goes for the Bible Code group. One may look for random patterns of letters making the correct word of prophecy even within the book Moby Dick. (That has actually been tried.)

2001 - Sep 18, 2001   Charles Taylor, the daddy of all false doomsday prophets, takes another swipe at it. The rapture will be on Rosh Hashanah. (Oropeza p.57)

2001 - Dec 8, 2001 - The author of "The Ninth Wave" web site was convinced that the Church would be raptured on this date, and people will explain the disappearance as alien abductions.

2001 - Pyramidologist Georges Barbarin, subscribing to the concept of the Great Week, predicted that Christ's Millennium would begin in 2001. (Mann p.118)

2001 - According to the Unarius Academy of Science, aliens they called "space brothers" were to land near El Cajon, California, ushering in a new age. When it did not occur their explanation was, "The Space Brothers have not landed because we, the people of Earth, are not ready to accept advanced peoples from another planet." (Heard p.26-27) Well duh! Some people can't even deal with advanced people in their own neighborhood.

2001 - Gordon-Michael Scallion predicted major earth changes taking place between 1998 and 2001, culminating in a pole shift. (Heard p.26-27)

2001 - Nation of Islam numerologist Tynetta Muhammad figured that 2001 would be the year of the End. (Weber p.213) Every religion has its fools.

2002 - The end of the world, according to Church Universal and Triumphant leader Elizabeth Clare Prophet, following a 12-year period of devastation and nuclear war. (Kyle p.156) Clare never missed a beat. People are still buying her books and listening to her dribble.

2002 – According to the doomsday list, "Charles R. Weagle's now-defunct website, warning2002ad.com predicted a "nuclear judgement" on the world's industrialized nations in 2002. (If those nations are doomed the other nations would die from fallout. Oops…)

2003 - May 5, 2003 - A UFO will pick up true believers on this date, according to the

Nuwaubians, a Georgia cult headed by Dr. Malachi Z. York, who claims to be the incarnation of God and a native of the planet Rizq. (Like in, "believing this guy is taking a risk.) (Time Magazine, July 12, 1999)

2003 - May 13, 2003 - Nancy Lieder of ZetaTalk believed that the "end time" will take place on this day with the approach of a giant planet known as the "12th Planet". This planet supposedly orbits the sun once every 3600 years. The planet will cause...you guessed it! A pole shift!! Ms. Lieder gives some information about this on her Troubled Times site. Just a note: According to Kepler's 3rd law of planetary motion: The ratio of the squares of the revolutionary periods for two planets is equal to the ratio of the cubes of their semimajor axes. Kepler's Third Law implies that the period for a planet to orbit the Sun increases rapidly with the radius of its orbit. Thus, we find that Mercury, the innermost planet, takes only 88 days to orbit the Sun but the outermost planet (Pluto) requires 248 years to do the same. A period of 3600 years places the planet 233 astronomical units from the Sun. To put this in perspective, Pluto is only 32.1 AUs from the sun. An astronomical unit is the mean distance between Earth and Sun. The rogue planet would be so far away it could not even distinguish the sun from any other star.

2003 - May 15, 2003 - A Japanese cult called Pana Wave, whose members dress in white, claimed that a mysterious 10th Planet would pass by Earth, causing its axis to tip. (Source: WWRN)

2003 - Nov 29, 2003 - The human race would all but wiped out by nuclear war between Oct 30 and

Nov 29, 2003, according to Aum Shinrikyo. (Alnor p.98) These guys are like the crabby uncle you never liked, who always talked about killing people in the war. (Call a friend to see if they were right.)

2004 Major world events beginning in August 1999 would lead to full-scale war in the year 2000, followed by a rebirth from the ashes in 2004, according to Taoist prophet Ping Wu.

2005 - Oct 4, 2005 - The end of the world, according to John Zachary in his 1994 book "Mysterious Numbers of the Sealed Revelation." The Tribulation was to begin on August 28, 1998. I'm sorry. You got the wrong number. (McIver #3477)

2004 - Oct 17, 2004 Clay Cantrell took the dimensions of Noah's Ark and through some of his own unique mathematics arrived at this day as the date of the Rapture.

2005 – This actually marks the beginning of the end, since we are now waiting for the death of Pope Benedict XVI for the prophecy of Malachy to take place. In 1143, St. Malachy prophesied that there would only be 112 more Popes left before the end of the world. Pope Benedict is the 111th, which means that the antichrist will be here in the early 21st century. According to Malachy, the last Pope will be named Peter of Rome. Now, As we

have learned, Malachy only gace us 111 Popes. An extra was snuck in by someone else. So, we could be looking down the barrel of the end of days right now. (Skinner p.74-75)

2005 - Oct 18, 2005 - The beginning of Christ's Millennium, according to Tom Stewart in his book 1998: "Year of the Apocalypse." The Rapture was to take place on May 31, 1998, and the return of Jesus on October 13, 2005. (McIver #3226)

2006 - An atomic holocaust started by Syria was to take place between the years 2000 and 2006, according to Michael Drosnin's book, " The Bible Codes" (O'Shea p.178). Here's an excerpt from Drosnin's discredited book: "I checked 'World War' and 'atomic holocaust' against all three ways to write each Hebrew year for the next 120 years. Out of 360 possible matches for each of the two expressions, only two years matched both - 5760 and 5766, in the modern calendar the years 2000 and 2006. Rips, a supposed expert on Bible Code, later checked the statistics for the matches of 'World War' and 'atomic holocaust' with those two years and agreed that the results were 'exceptional.'"

2006 - The British cult, The Family, believed the end will come in 2006.

2007 - Apr 29, 2007 - In his 1990 book, "The New Millennium", Pat Robertson suggests this date as the day of Earth's destruction. (Abanes p.138)

2007 - Aug 2007 - Thomas Chase uses an incredible mishmash of Bible prophecy, numerology, Y2K, Bible codes, astrology, Cassini paranoia, Antichrist speculation, news events, New Age mysticism, the shapes of countries, Hale-Bopp comet timing, and more to show that Armageddon will happen around the year 2007, perhaps in August of that year.

2008 - Apr 6, 2008 - The beginning of Christ's millennial reign, according to Philip B. Brown.

2009 - According prophetess Lori Adaile Toye of the "I AM America Foundation," a series of Earth changes beginning in 1992 and ending in 2009 will cause much of the world to be submerged, and only 1/3 of America's population will survive. You can even order a map of the flooded USA from her website!

2010 - The final year according to the Hermetic Order of the Golden Dawn. (Shaw p.223)

2011 - Another possible date for Earth's entry into the Photon Belt. (See the May 5, 1997 entry)

2011 - Dec 31, 2011 - In an interesting parallel to the Harmonic Convergence concept, Solara Antara Amaa-ra, leader of the "11:11 Doorway" movement, claims that there's a "doorway of opportunity" lasting from January 11, 1992 to December 31, 2011 in which humanity is given the final chance to rid itself of evil and attain a higher level of consciousness, or doom will strike. (Wojcik p.206)

2012 James T. Harmon's Rapture prediction #3. (Oropeza p.89)

2012- Dec 21, 2012 - Terence McKenna combines Mayan chronology with a New Age pseudoscience called "Novelty Theory" to conclude that the collision of an asteroid or some "trans-dimensional object" with the Earth, or alien contact, or a solar explosion, or the transformation of the Milky Way into a quasar, or some other "ultranovel" event will occur on this day.

Dec 23, 2012- The end of the age, and some say the end of the world, according to the ancient Mayan calendar. (Abanes p.342)

2012 - NASA recently published a report detailing new magnetism on the Sun that will probably result in Major Solar Changes and destruction of satellite communications, GPS, Air Traffic, and Power Grids.

The report clearly states that a new Solar Cycle is possible resulting from a knot of magnetism that popped over the sun's eastern limb on Dec. 11th. 2007.

The report goes on to mention specific years

which major Earthly impact will be seen. The exact quote which mentions these years states;
"Many forecasters believe Solar Cycle 24 will be big and intense. Peaking in 2011 or 2012, the cycle to come could have significant impacts on telecommunications, air traffic, power grids and GPS systems. In this age of satellites and cell phones, the next solar cycle could make itself felt as never before." A solar mass ejection pointed at the earth could easily destroy our ozone and lay us open to the sun's radiation and the solar winds. Our atmosphere would be swept away and earth would become like the planet Mars.

Joseph Lumpkin

More books from Fifth Estate Publishing may be found at:
http://www.fifthestatepub.com

The Books of Enoch: A Complete Volume Containing 1
Enoch (The Ethiopic Book of Enoch), 2 Enoch (The Slavonic
Secrets of Enoch), 3 Enoch (The Hebrew Book of Enoch)
by Joseph Lumpkin
ISBN-13: 978-1933580807

Lost Books of the Bible: The Great Rejected Texts
by Joseph Lumpkin
ISBN-13: 978-1933580661

The Encyclopedia of Lost and Rejected Scriptures: The
Pseudepigrapha and Apocrypha
by Joseph Lumpkin
ISBN-13: 978-1933580913

The Gospel of Thomas: A Contemporary Translation
ISBN: 0976823349

Dark Night of the Soul - A Journey to the Heart of God
ISBN: 0974633631

The Book of Jubilees; The Little Genesis, The Apocalypse of
Moses
ISBN: 1933580097

224